This is the most stress-relieving coloring book you'd ever tried!

It contains 30 unique designs with Animals, Birds, Flowers, Travel Objects and more.

Use any one color to find out, what is hidden by mystery spots!

Every picture will SURPRISE you!

Copyright © 2020 by Sunlife Drawing
All rights reserved

No part of this publication may be reproduced, distributed, or transmitted in any form or by any means, including photocopying, recording, or other electronic or mechanical methods, without the prior written permission of the author, except in the case of brief quotations embodied in critical reviews and certain other noncommercial uses permitted by copyright law.
mail@sunlifedrawing.com

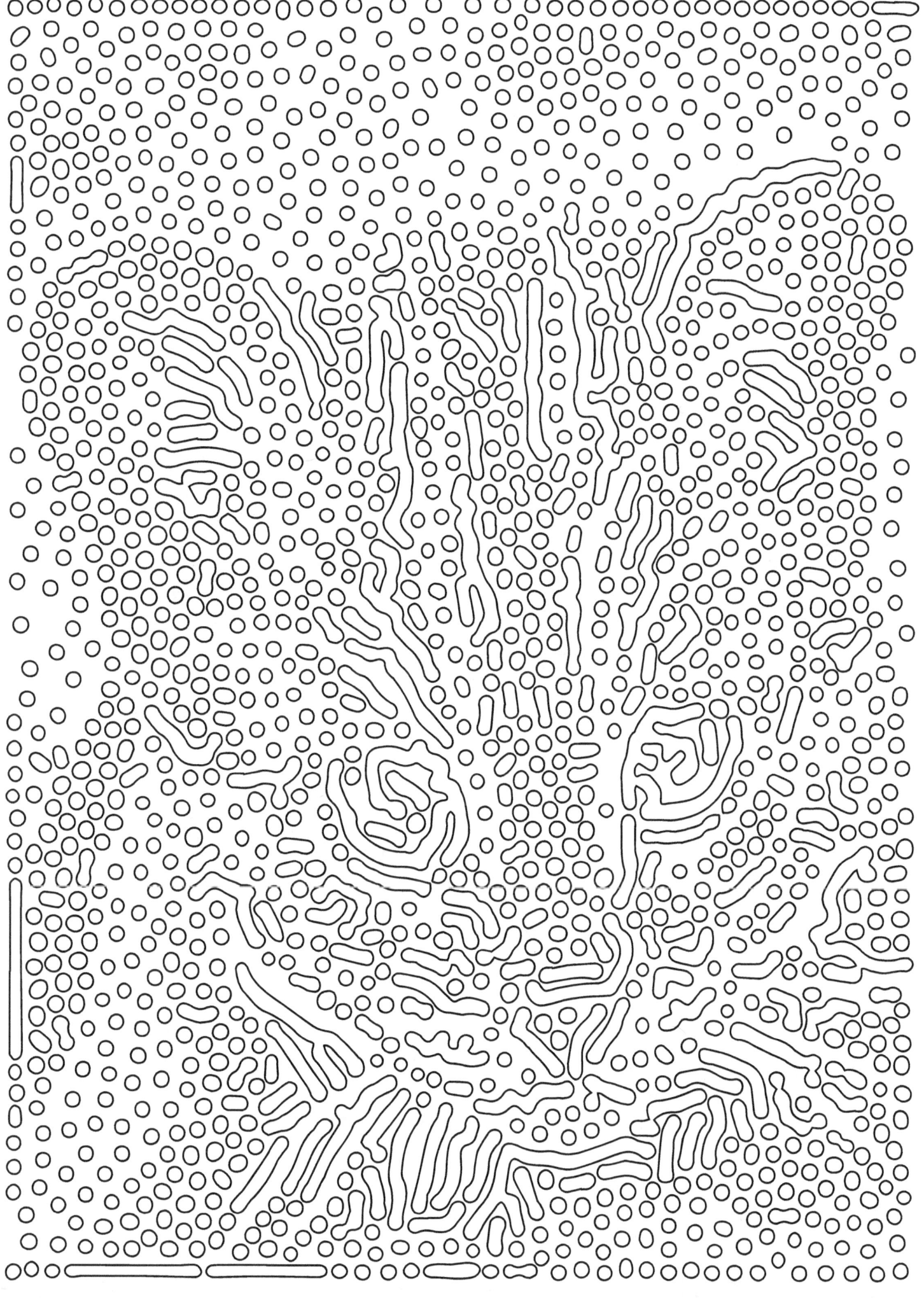

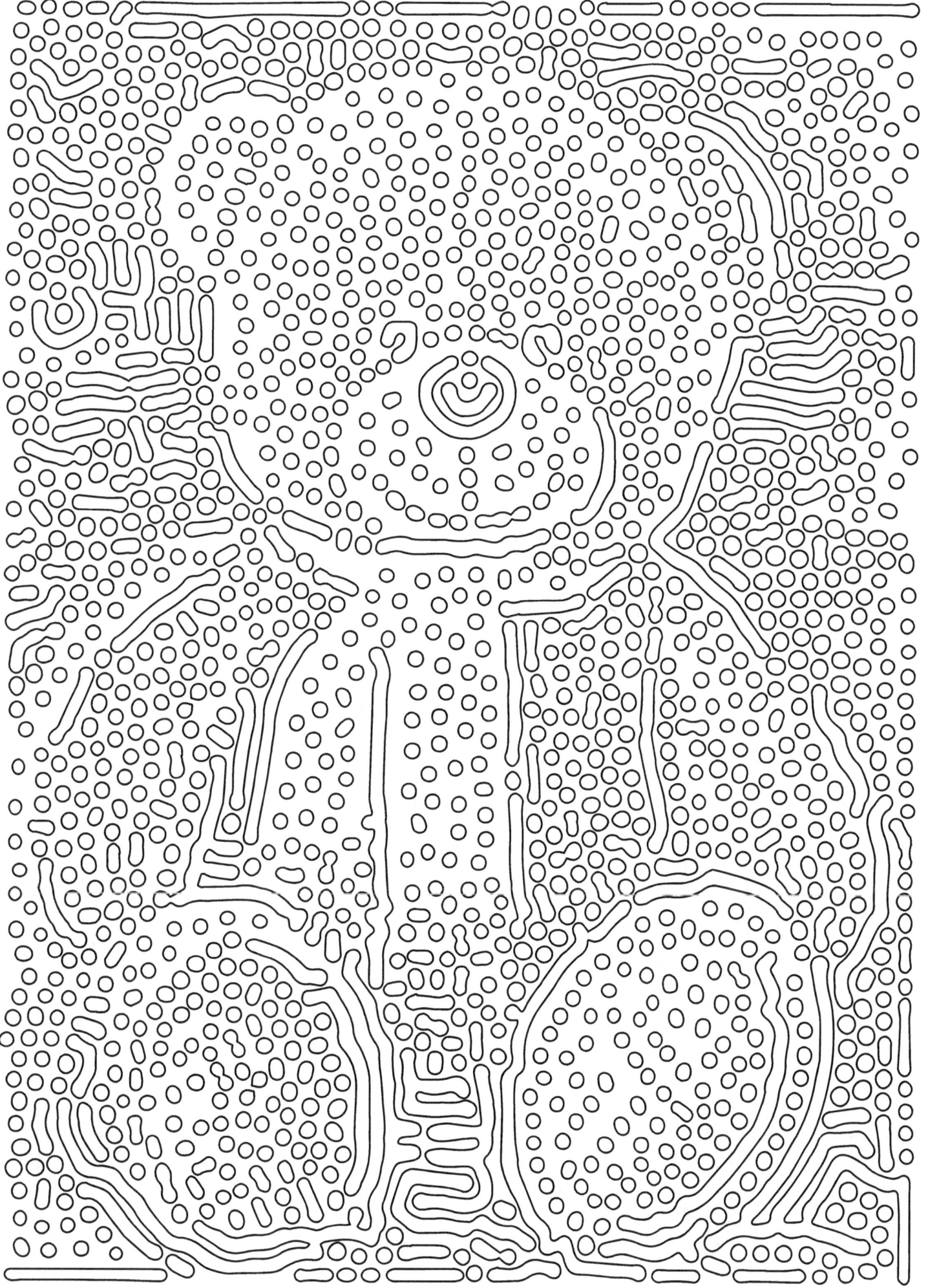

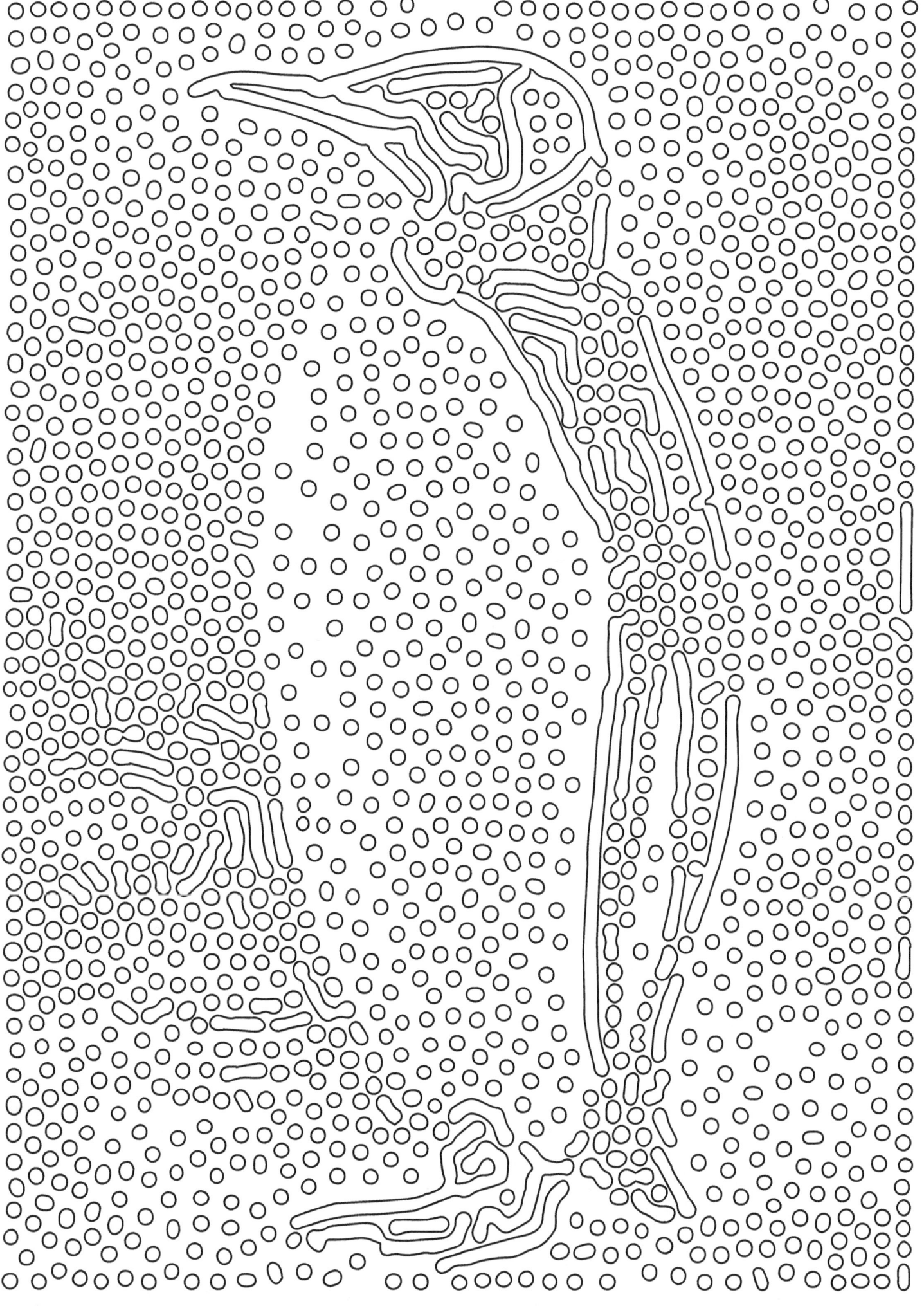

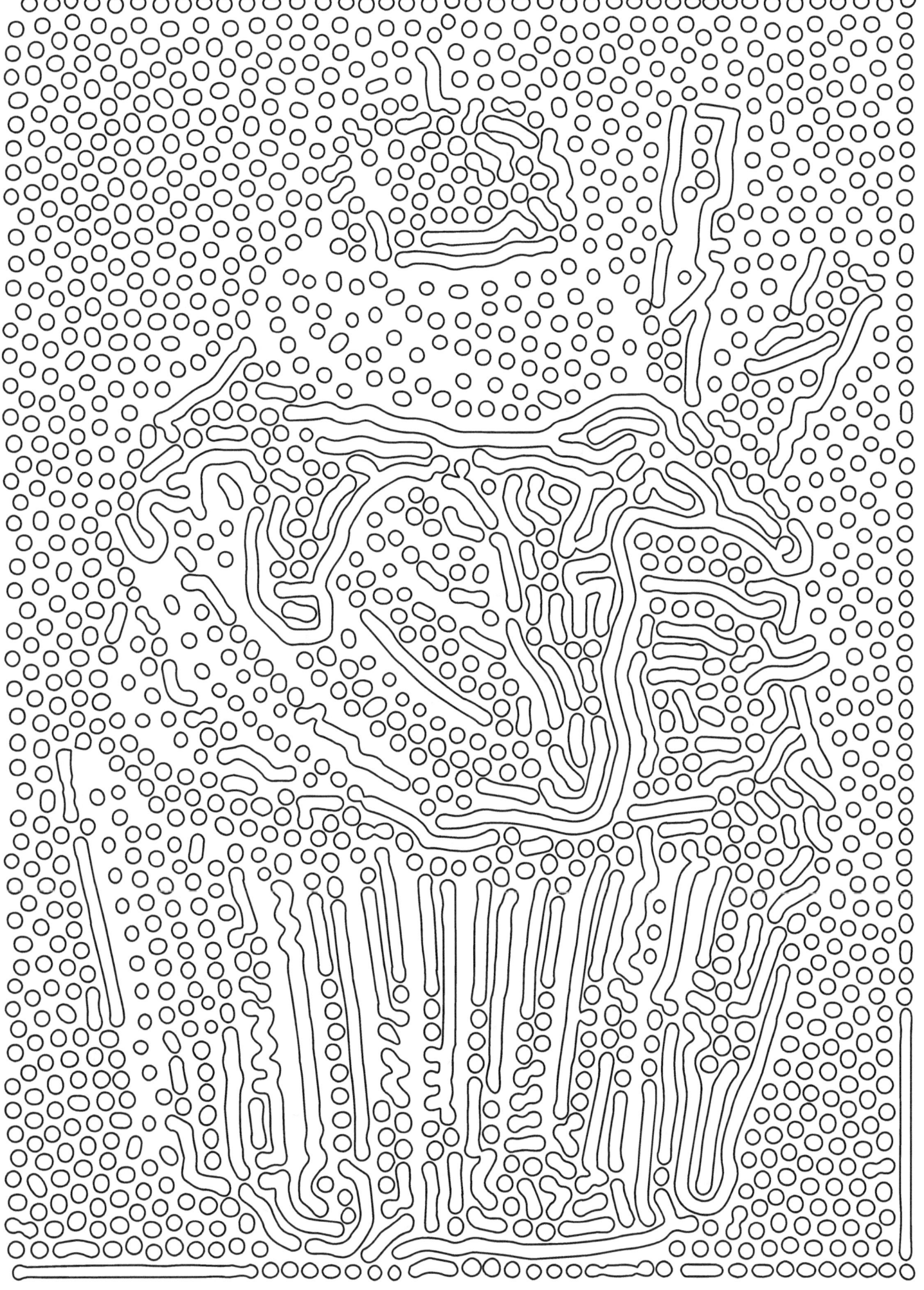

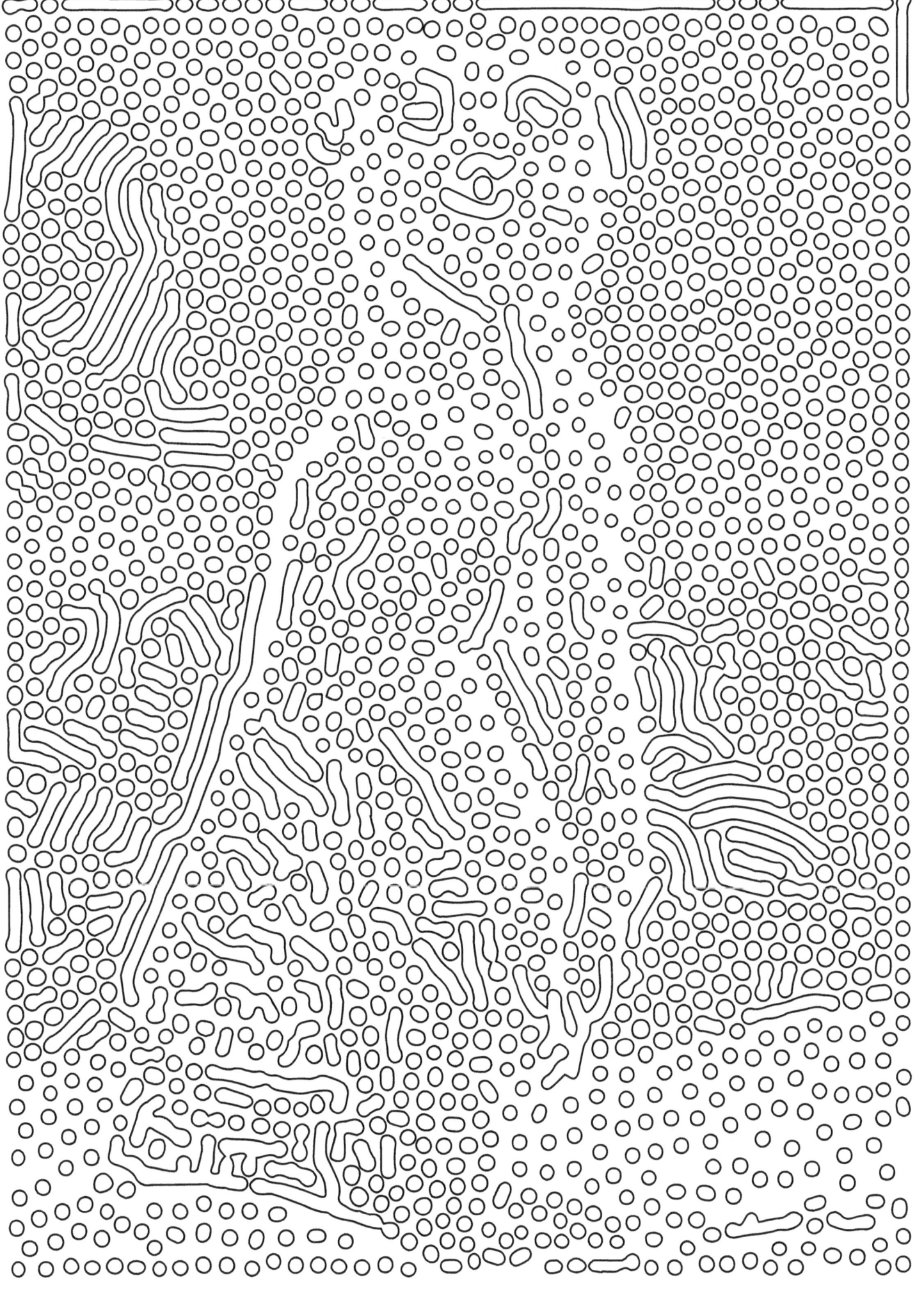

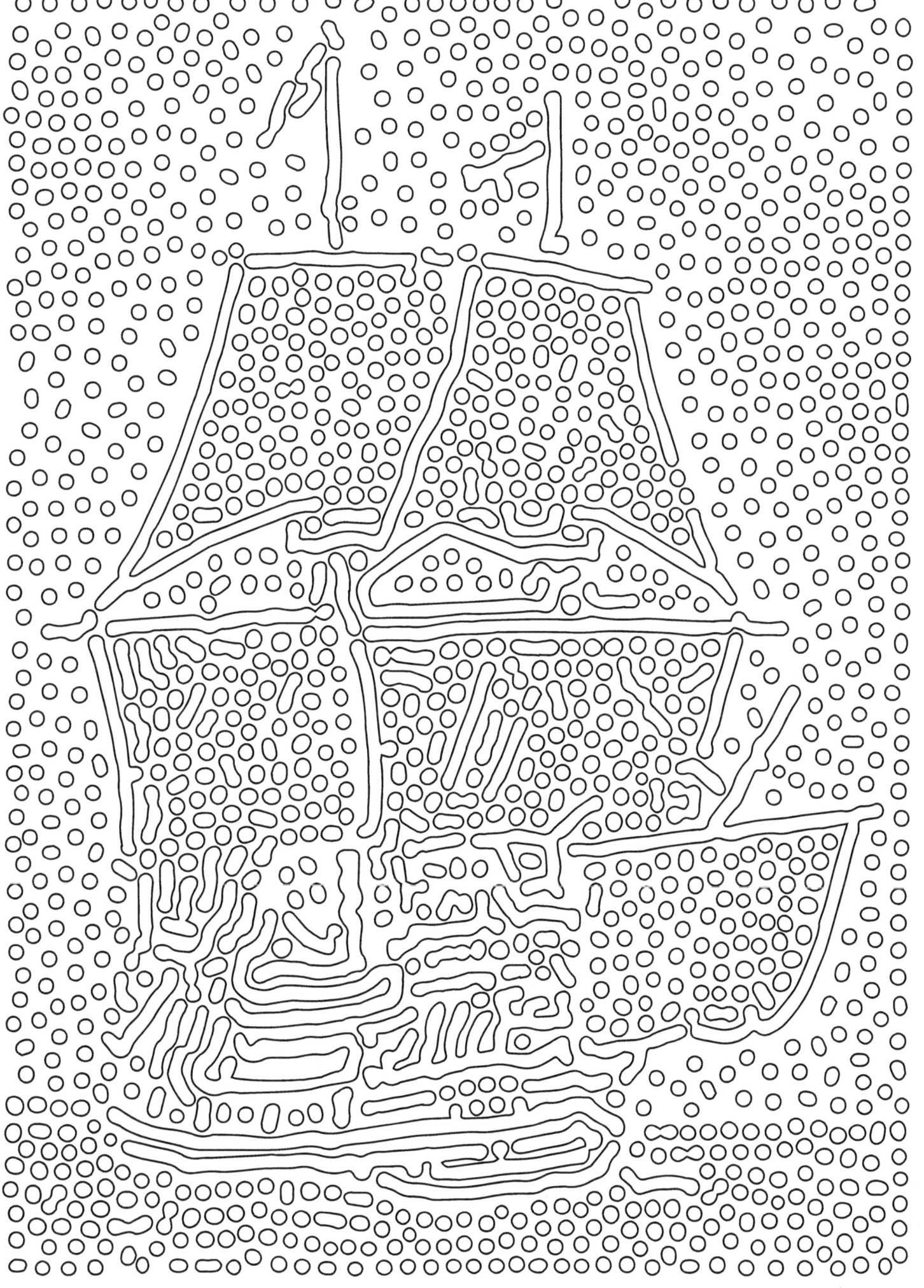

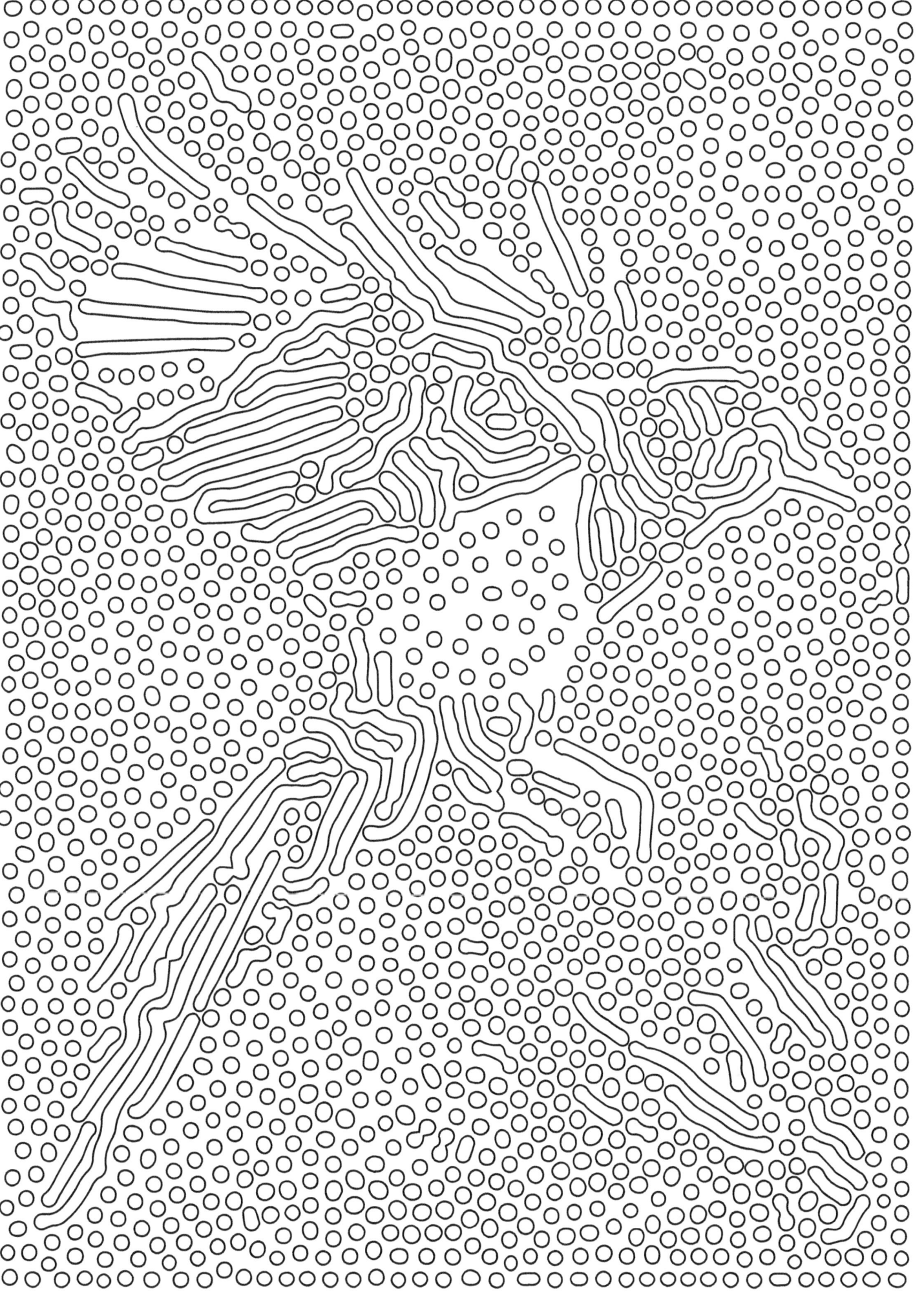

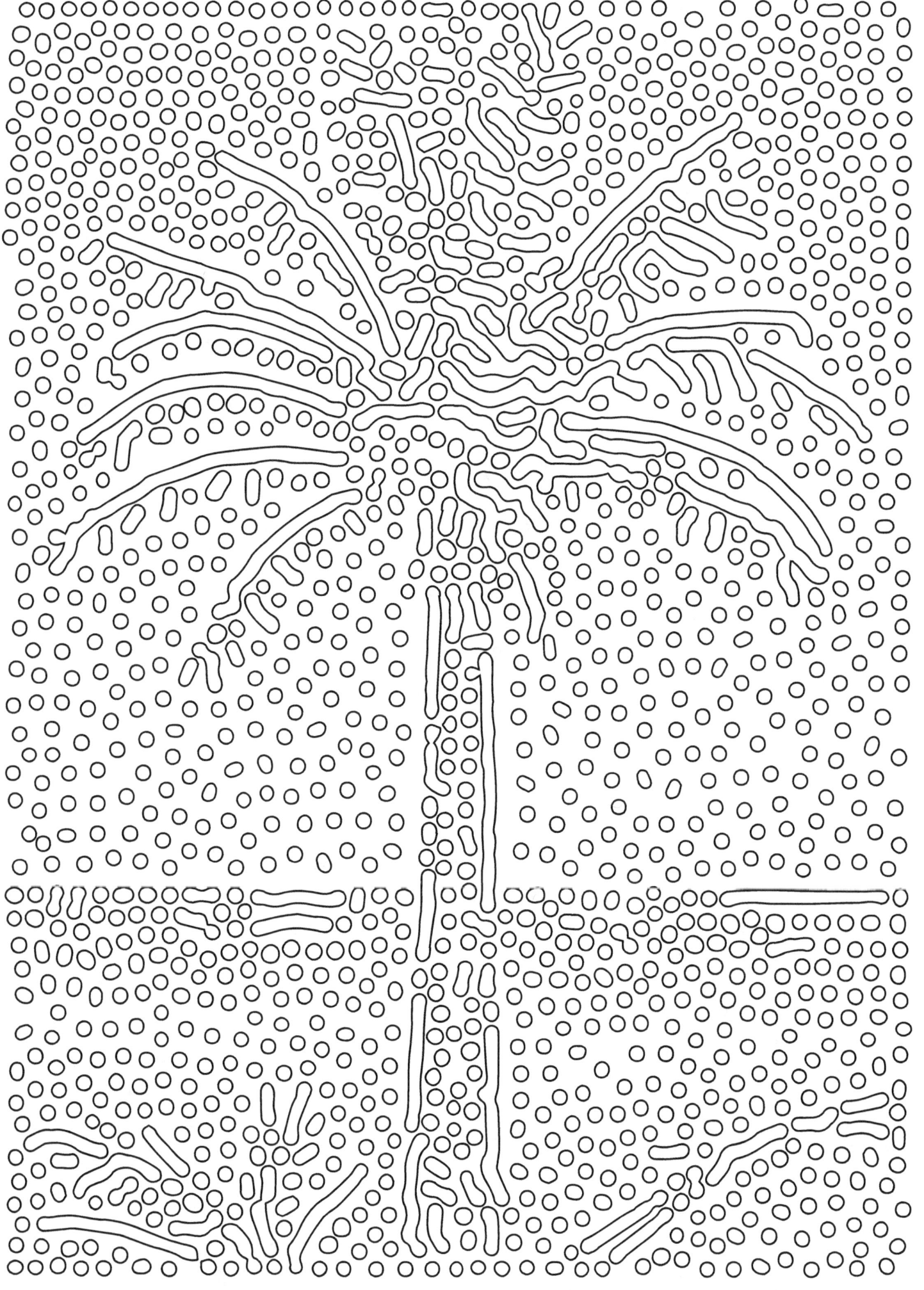

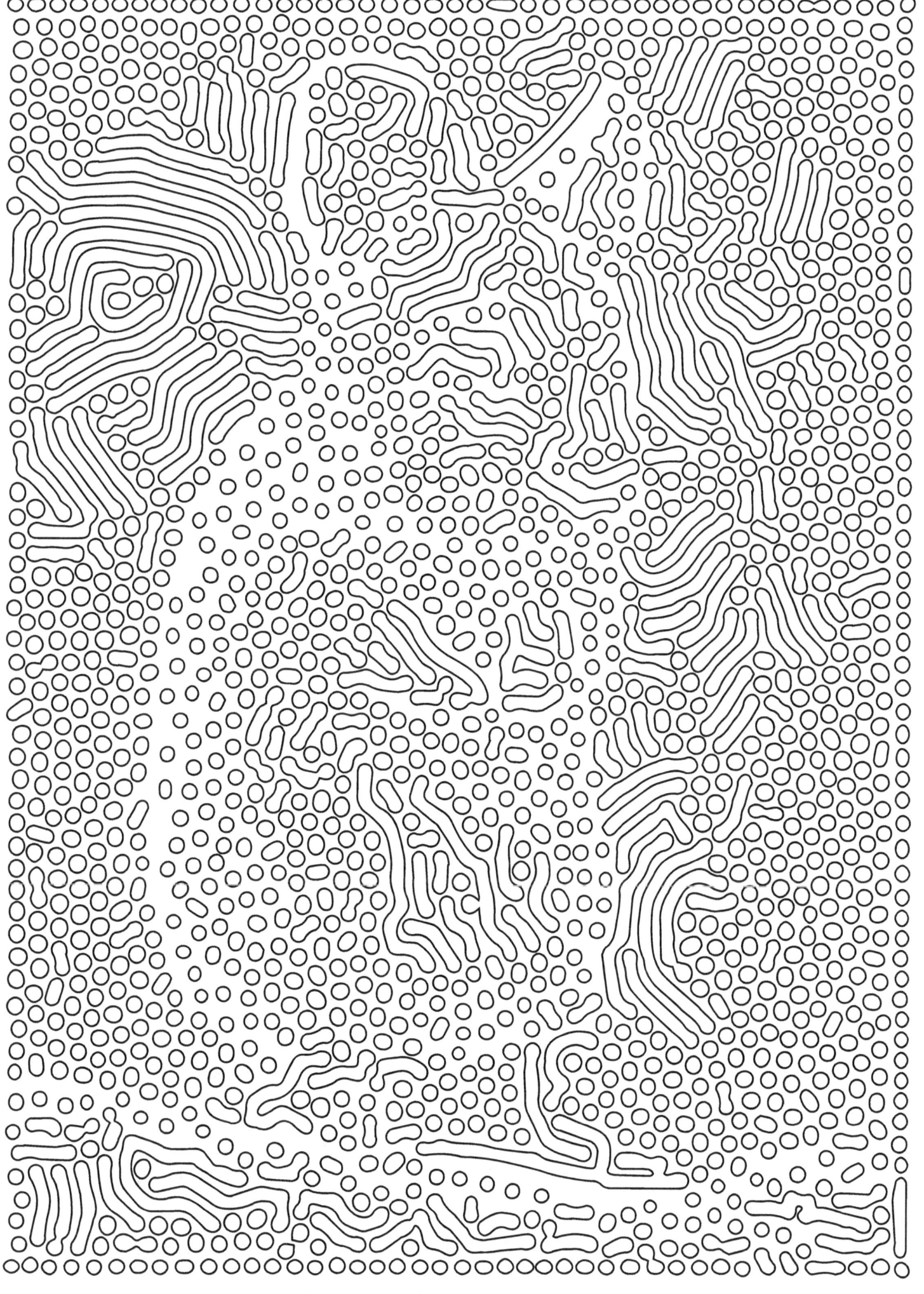

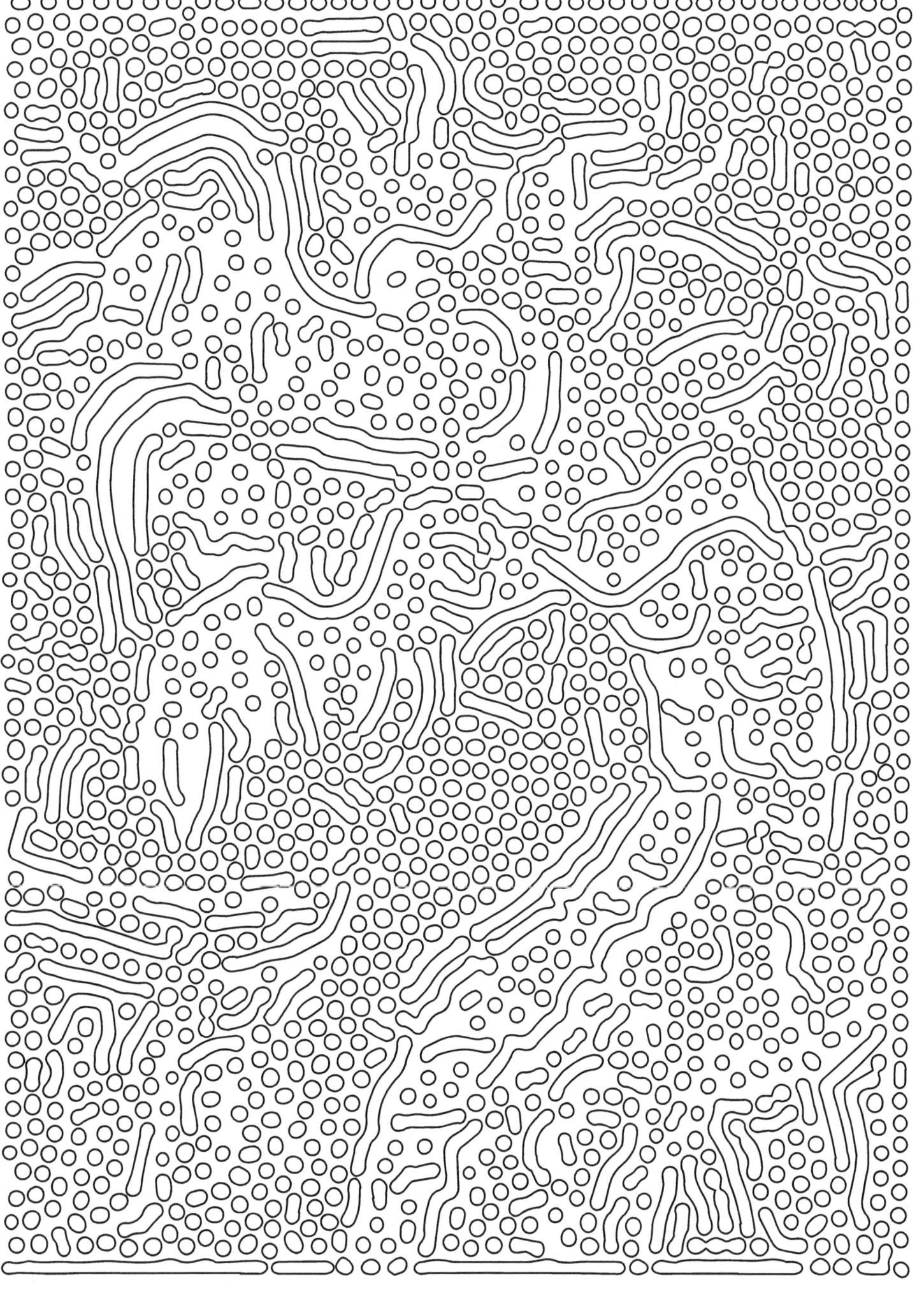

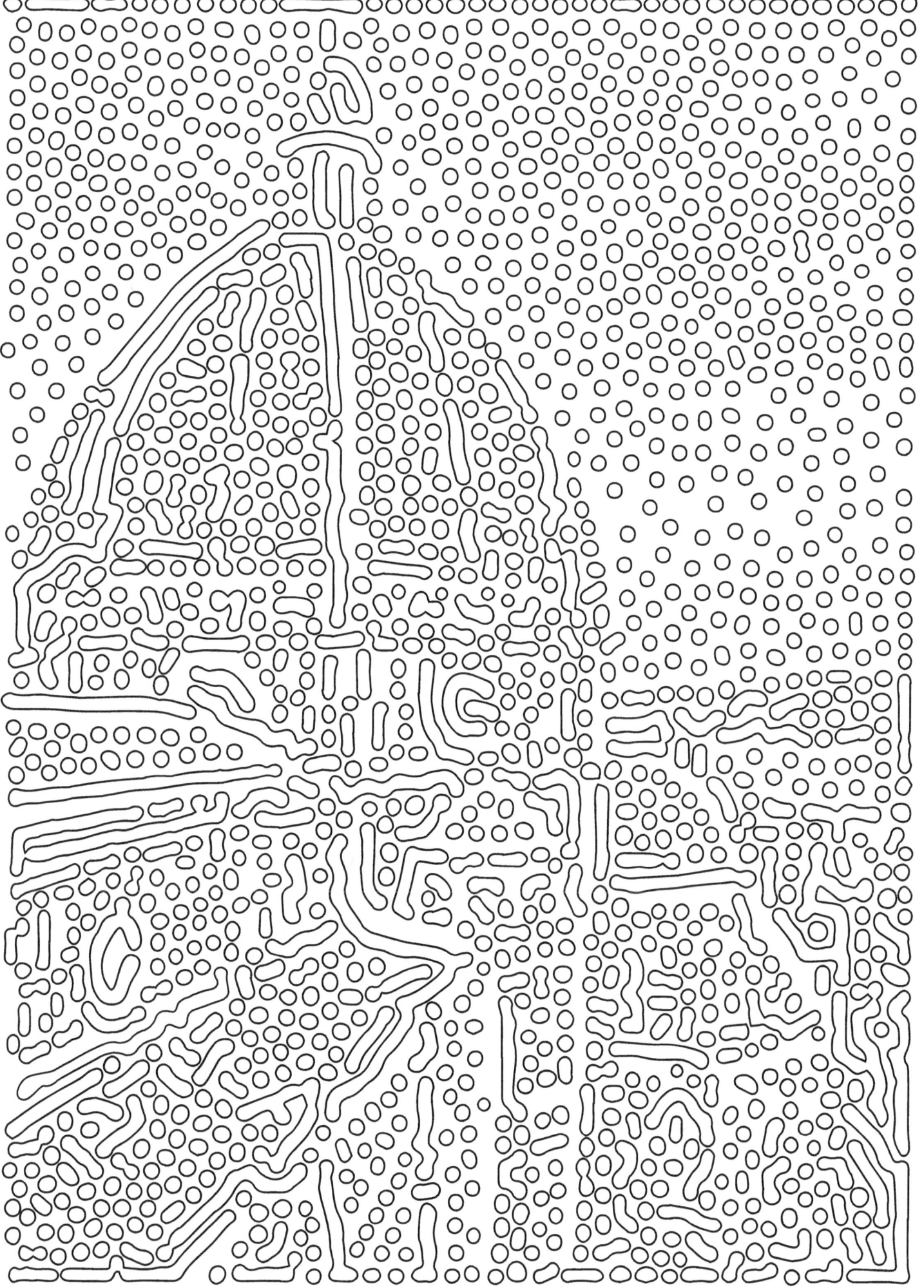

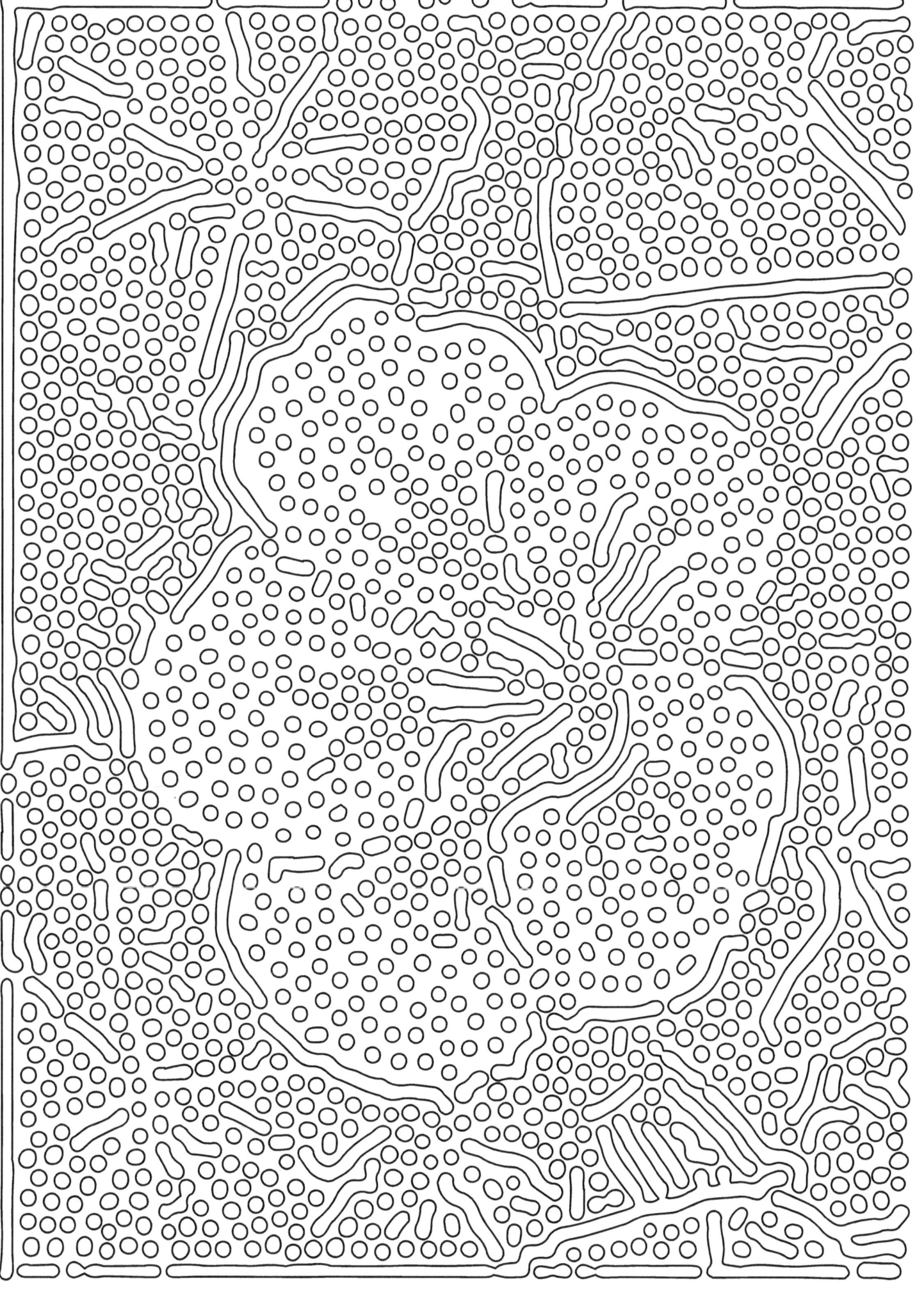

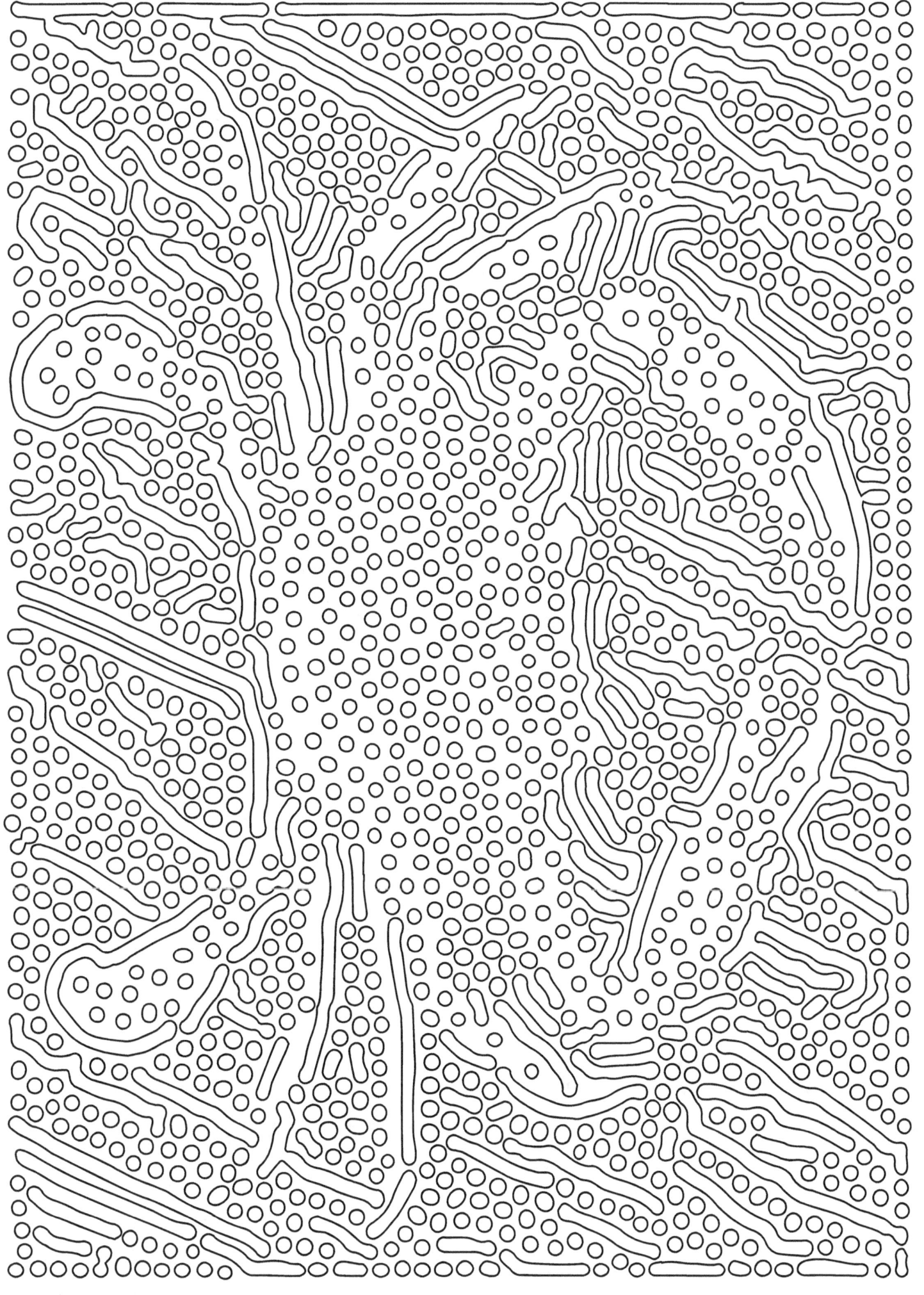

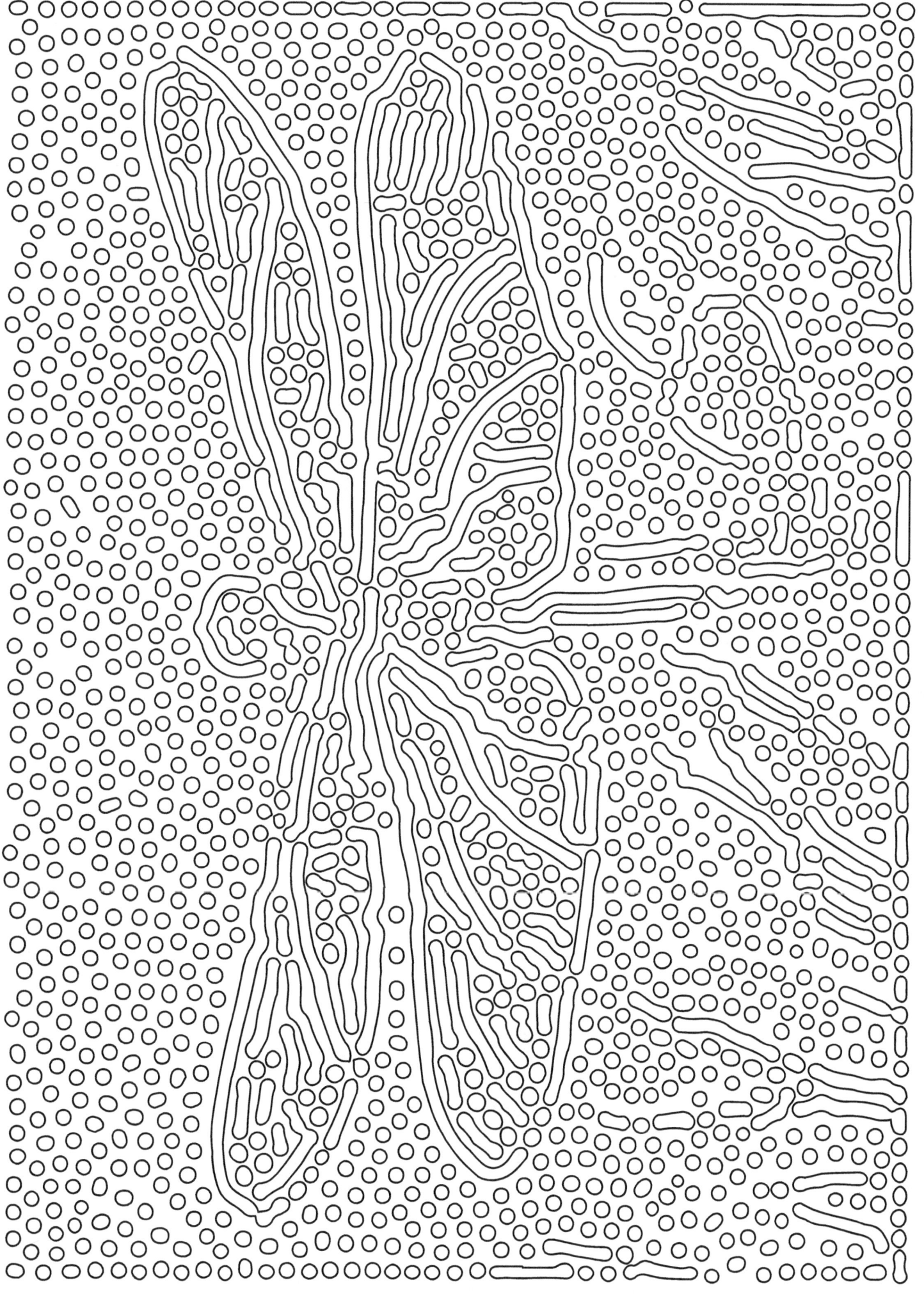

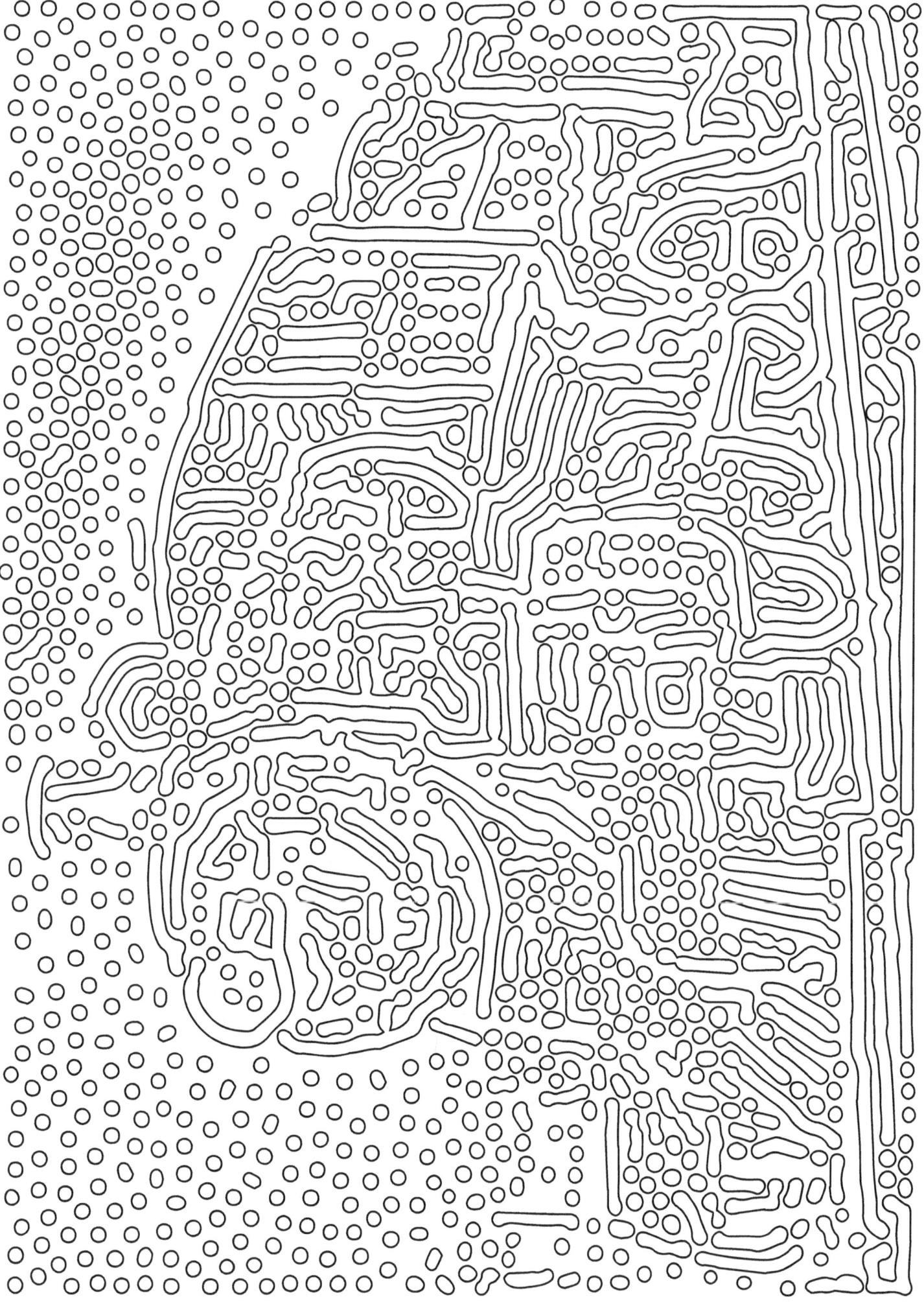

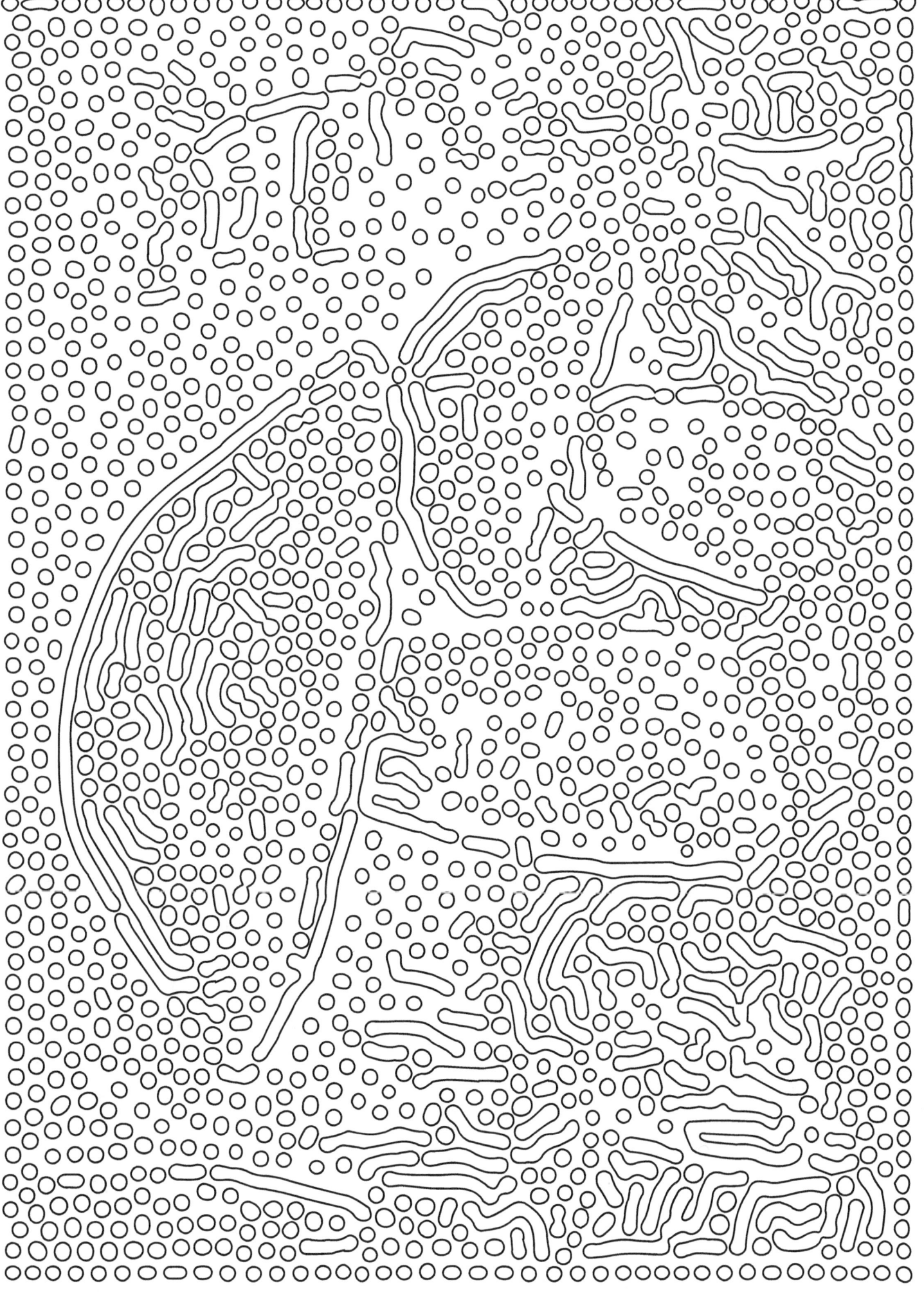

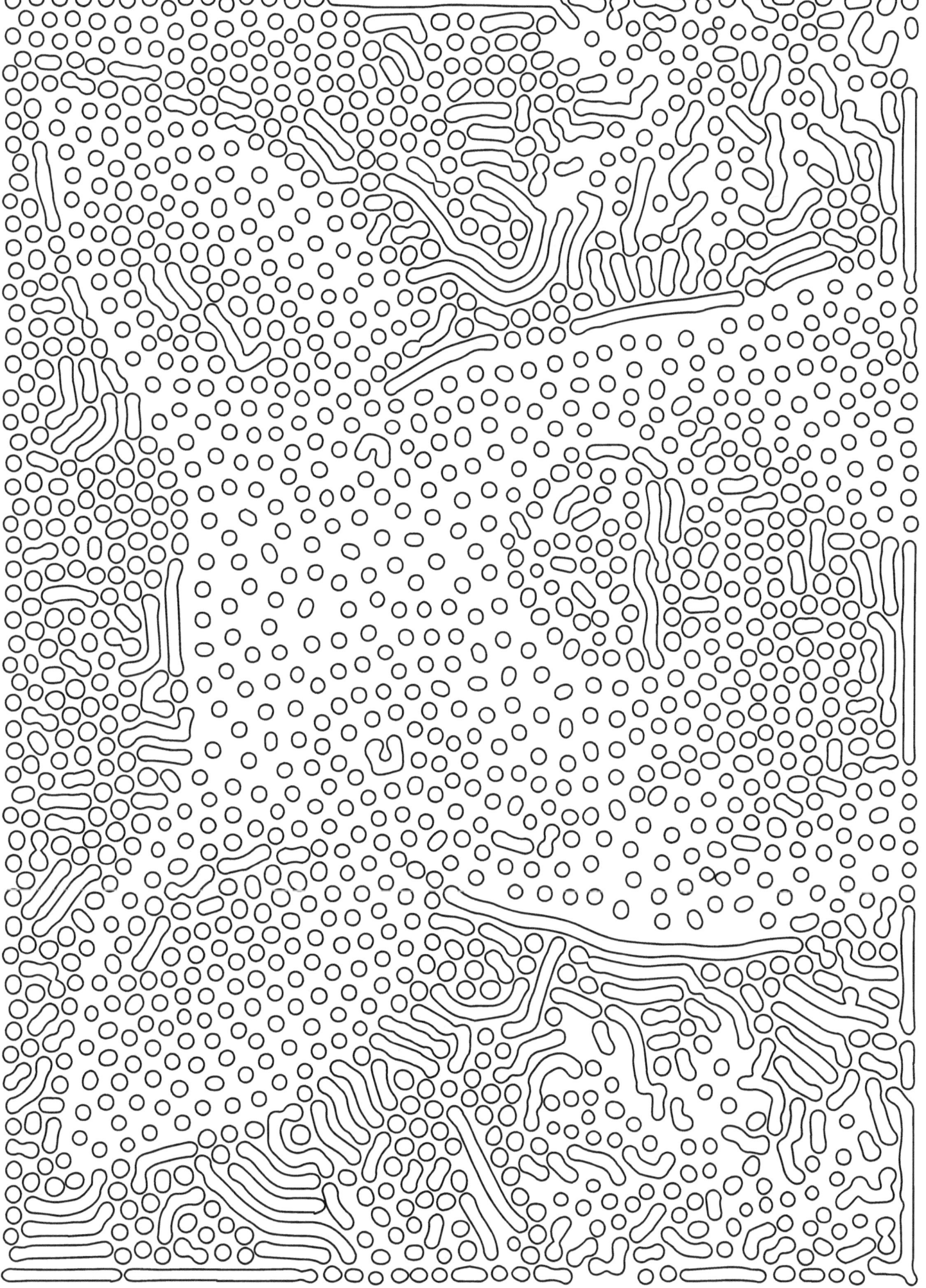

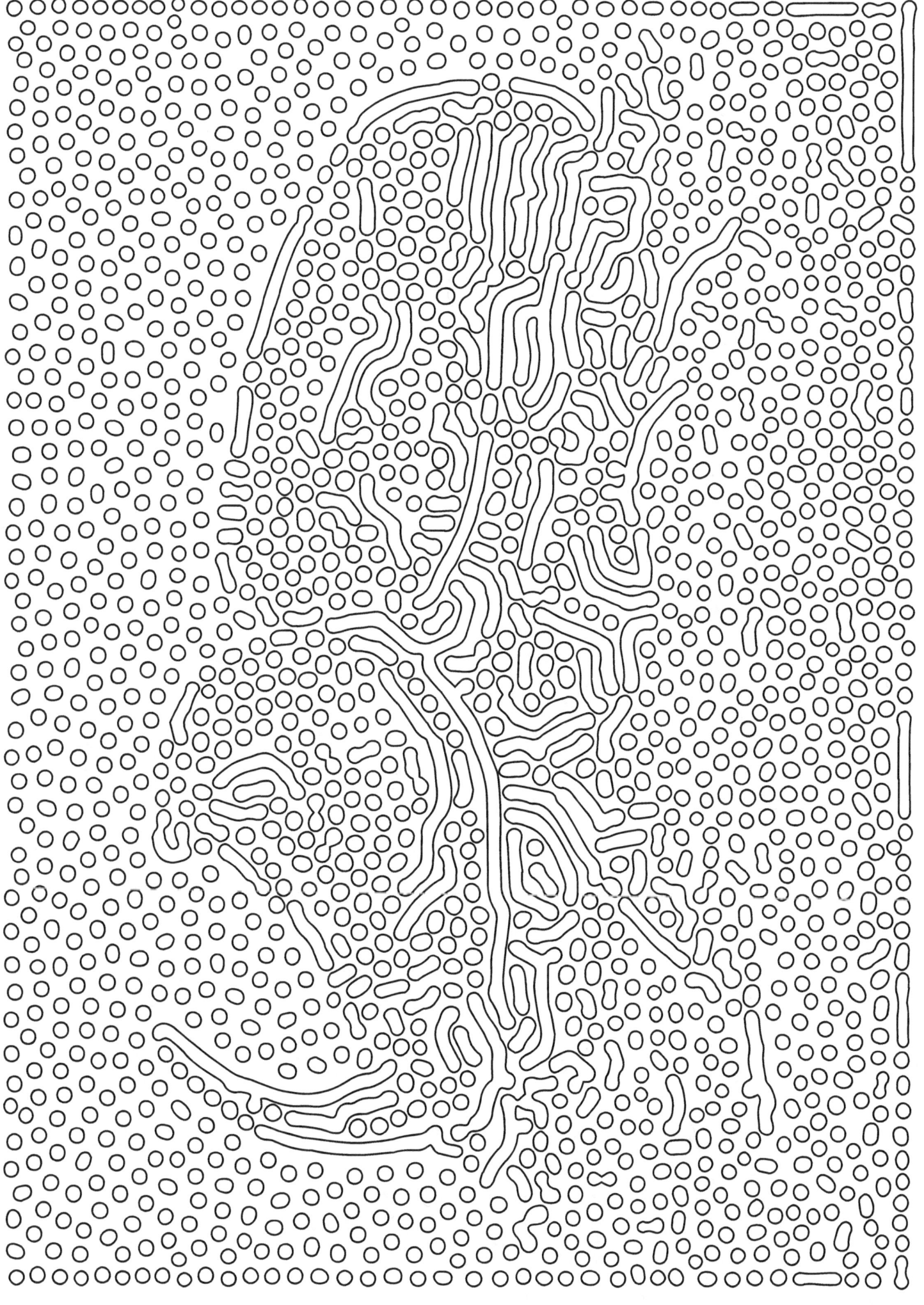

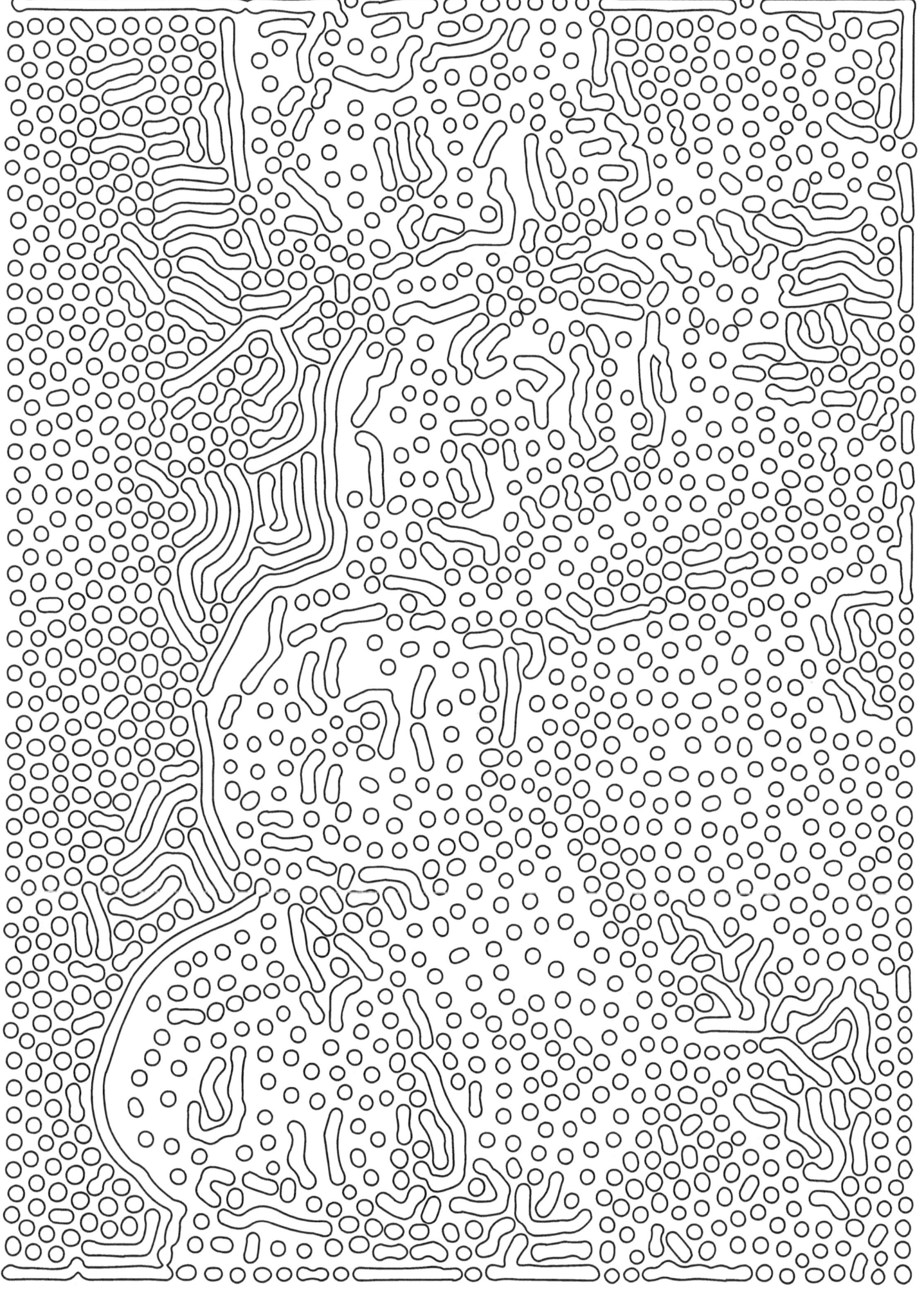

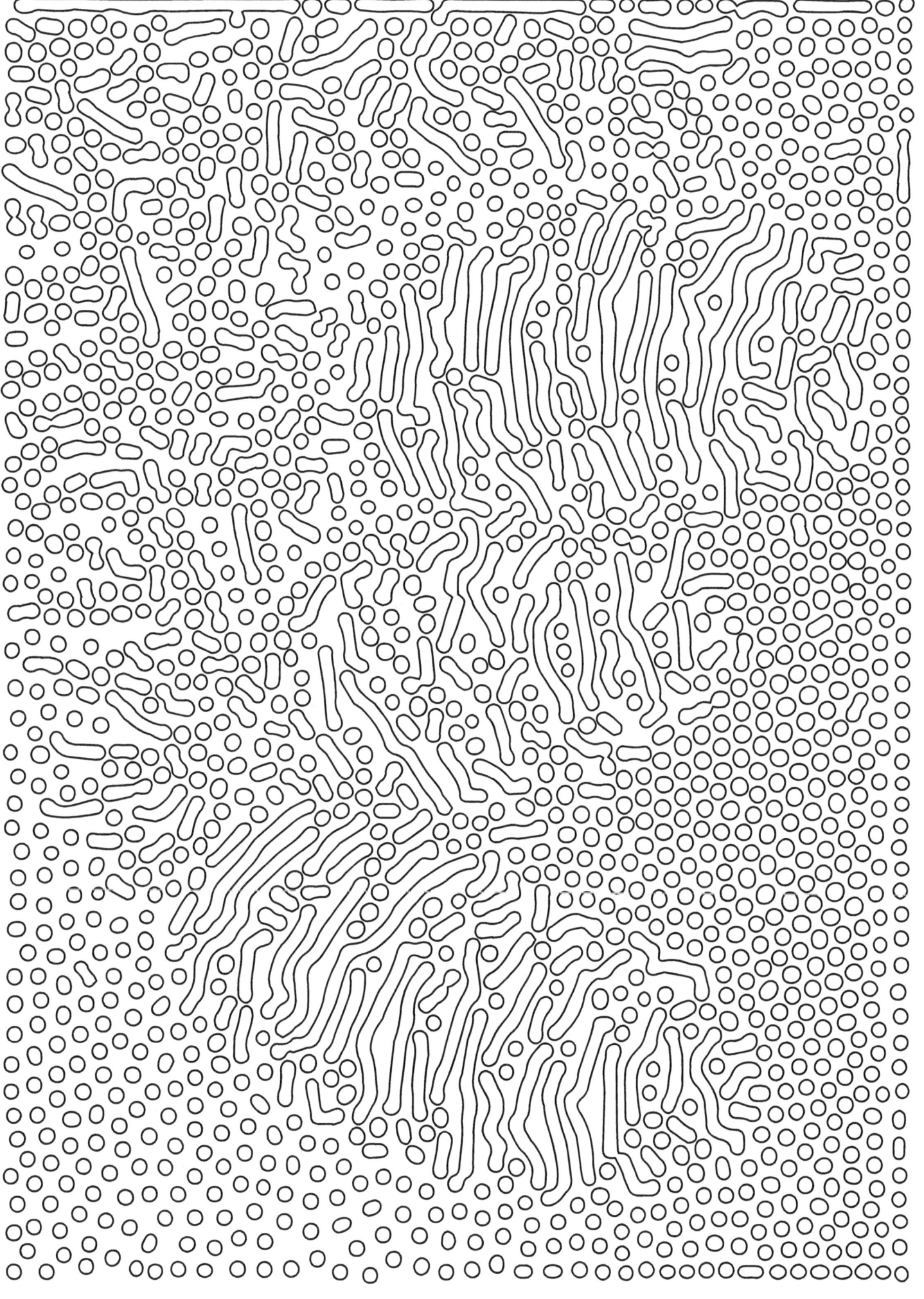

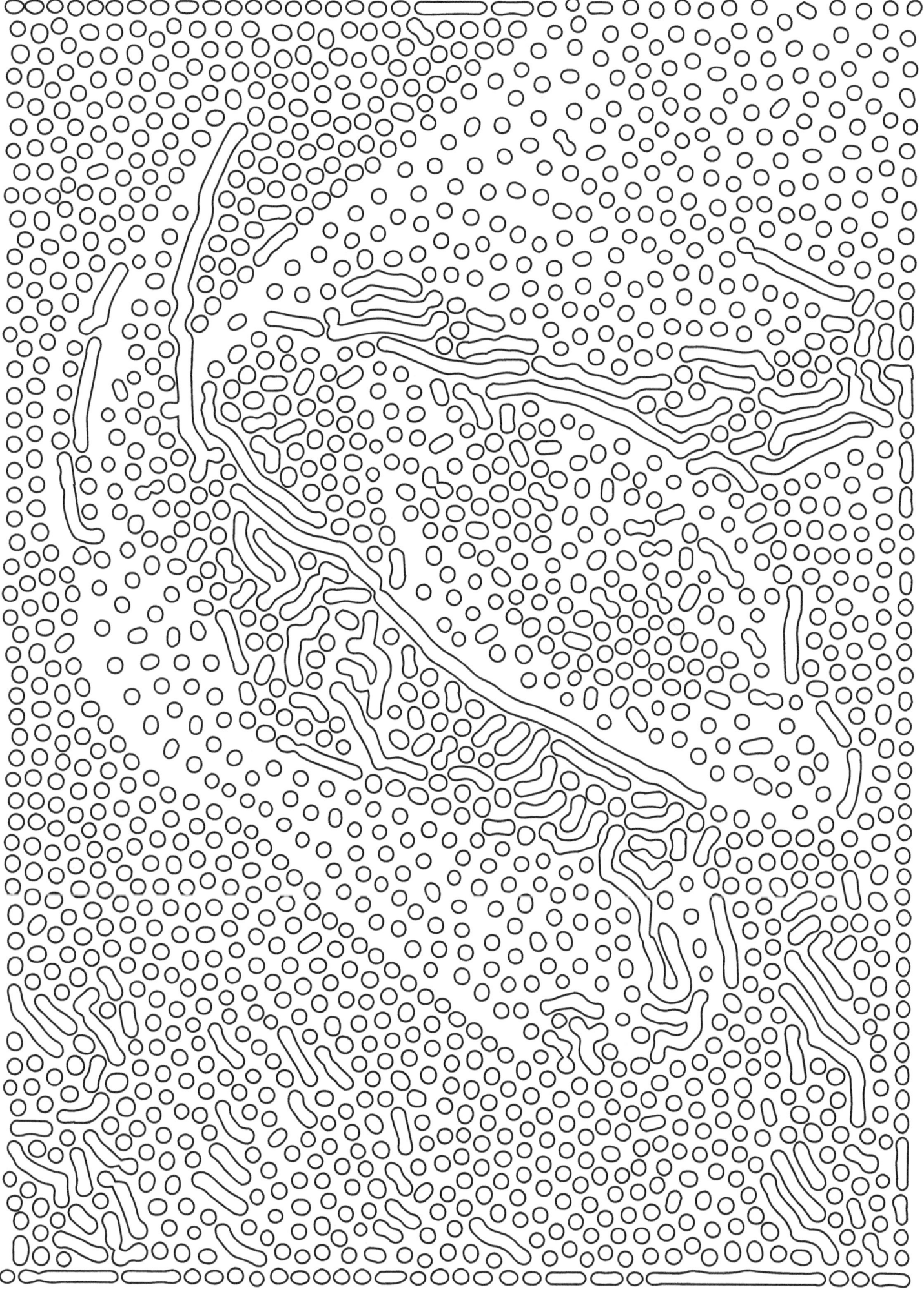

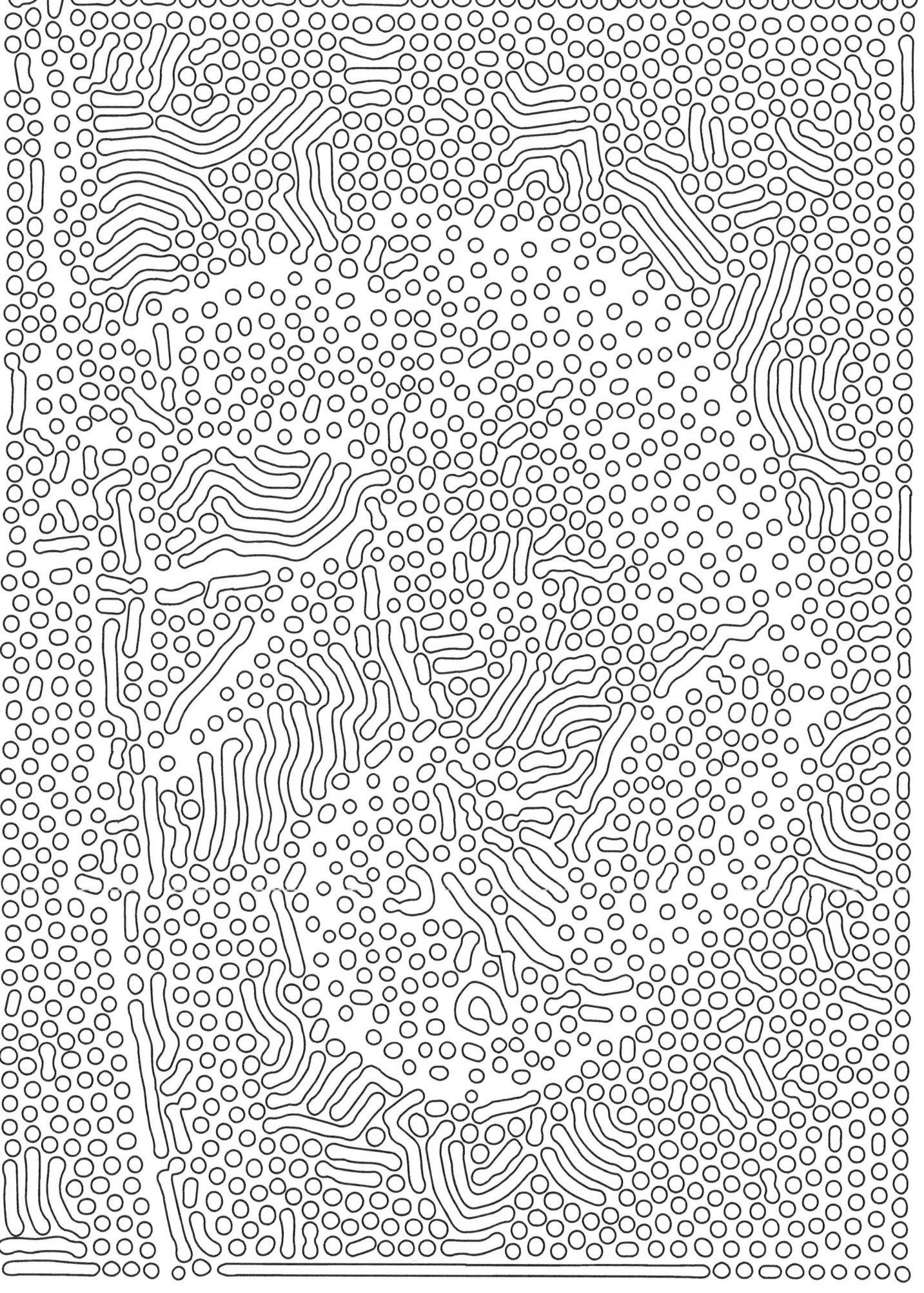

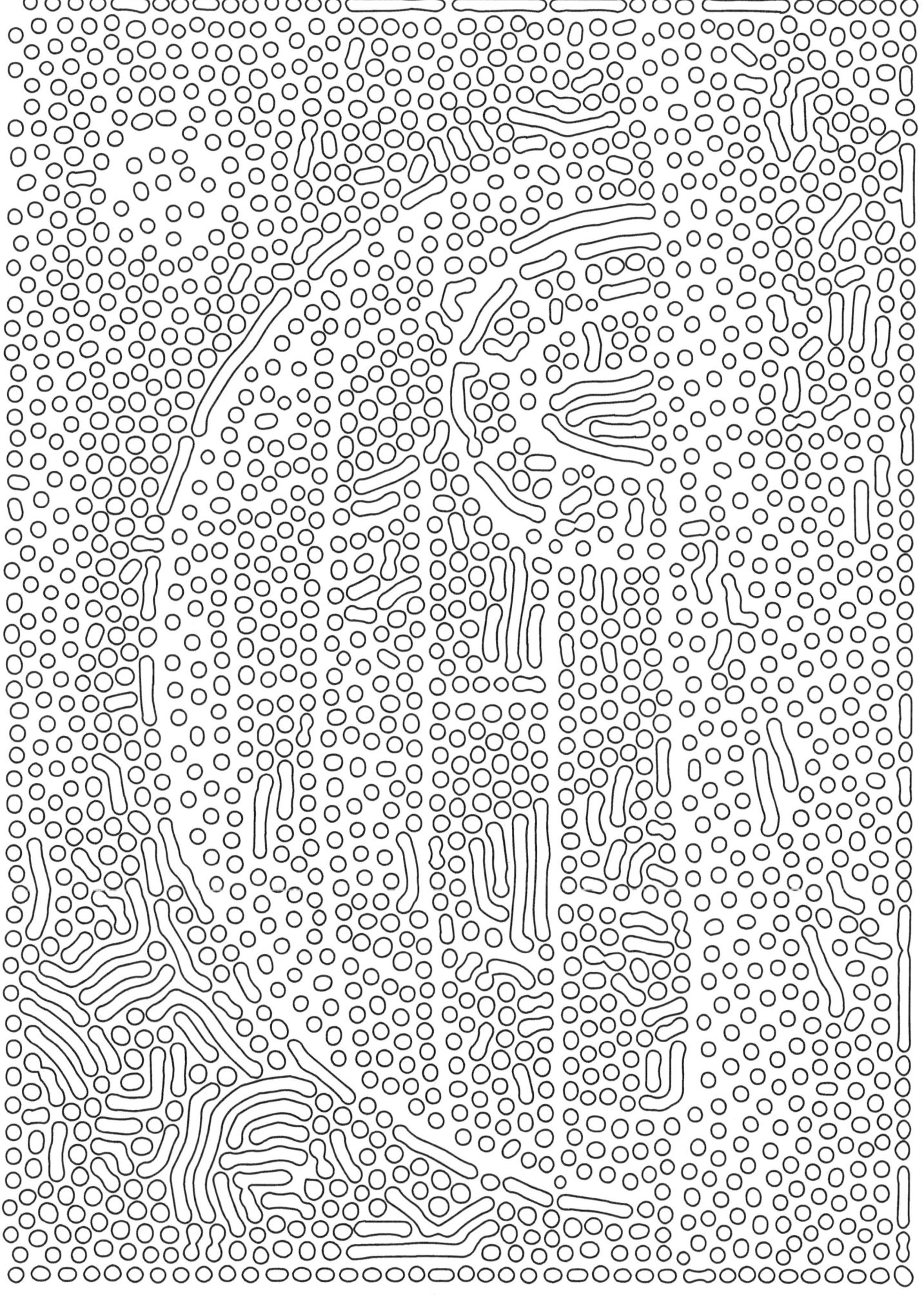

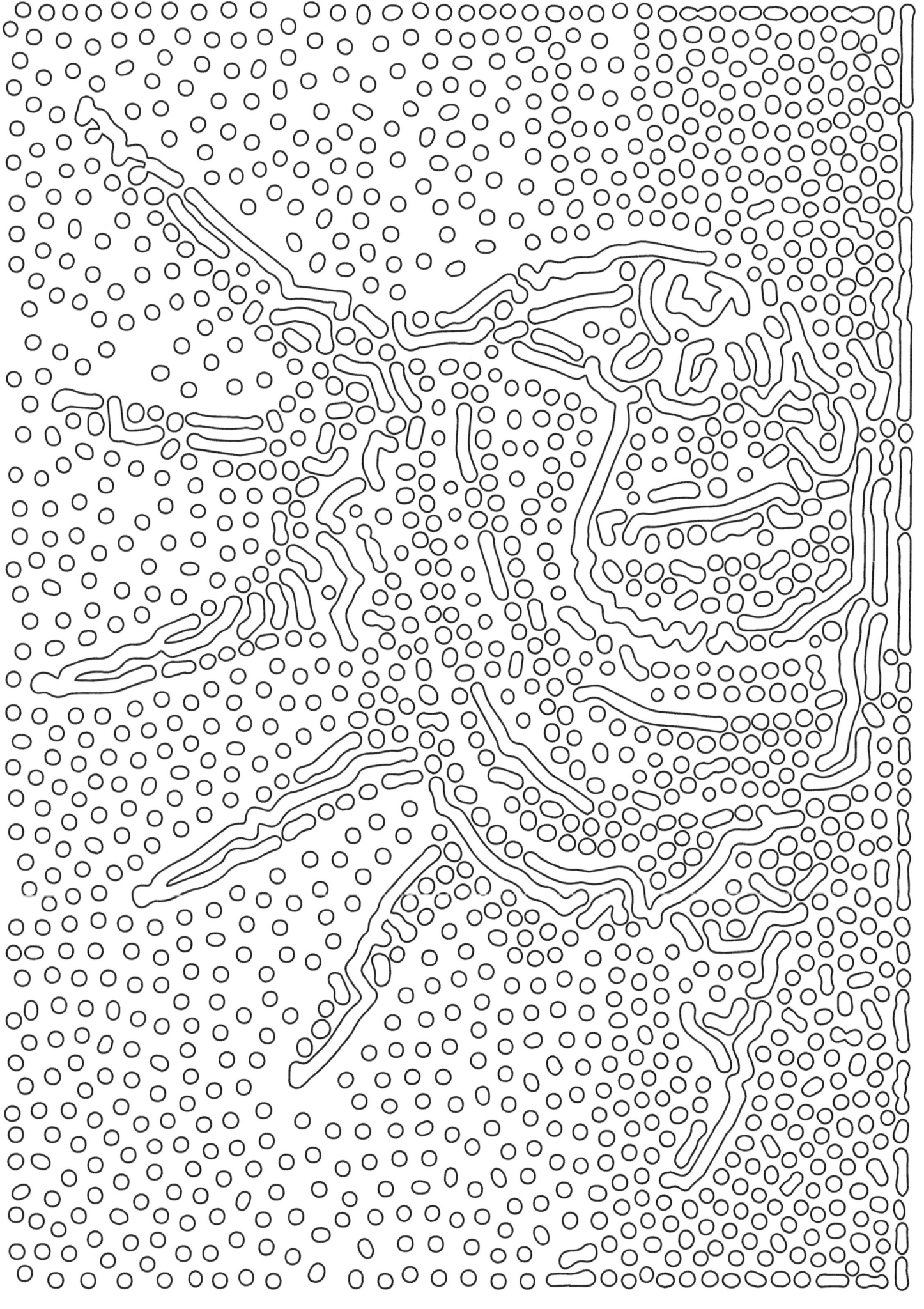

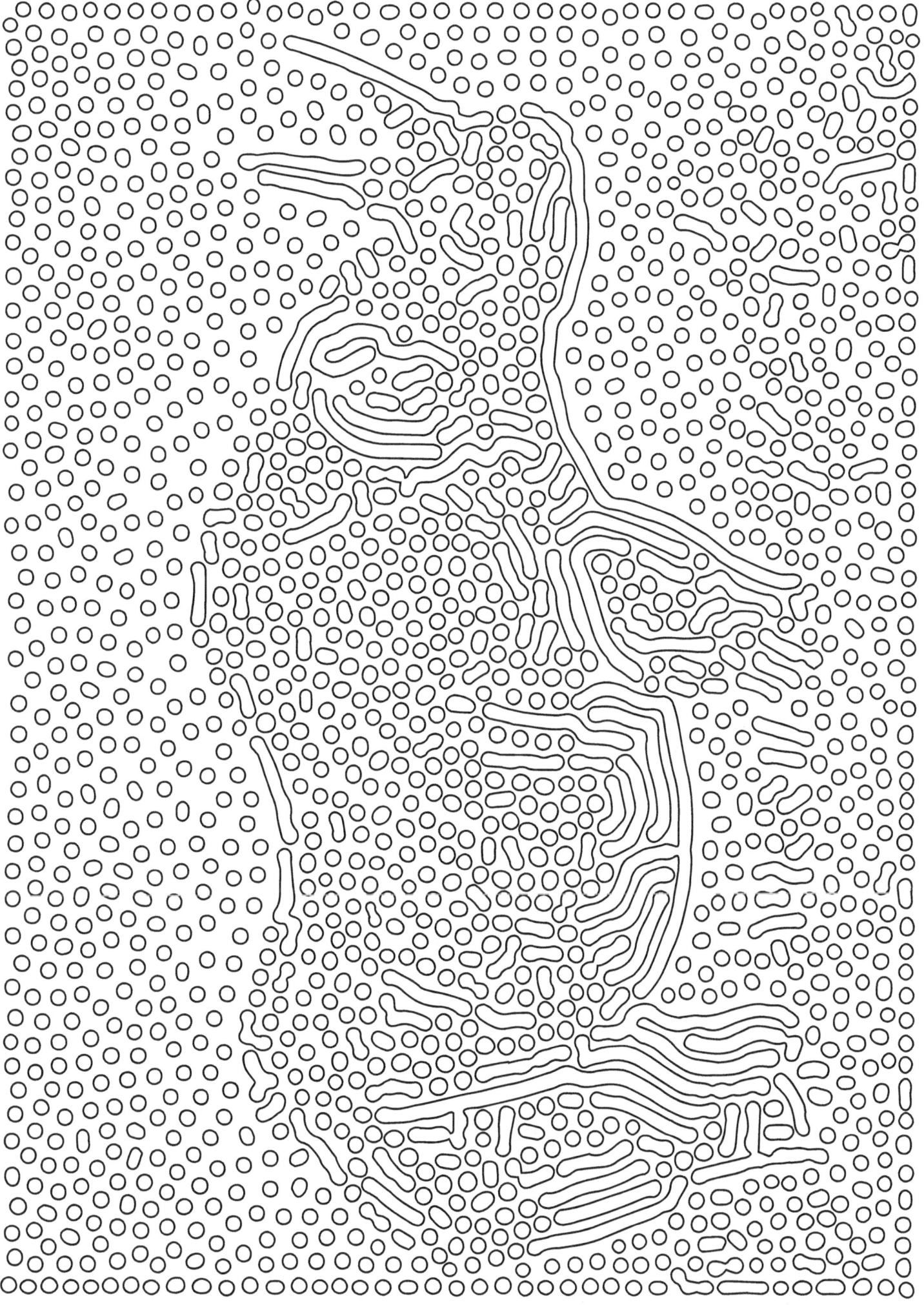

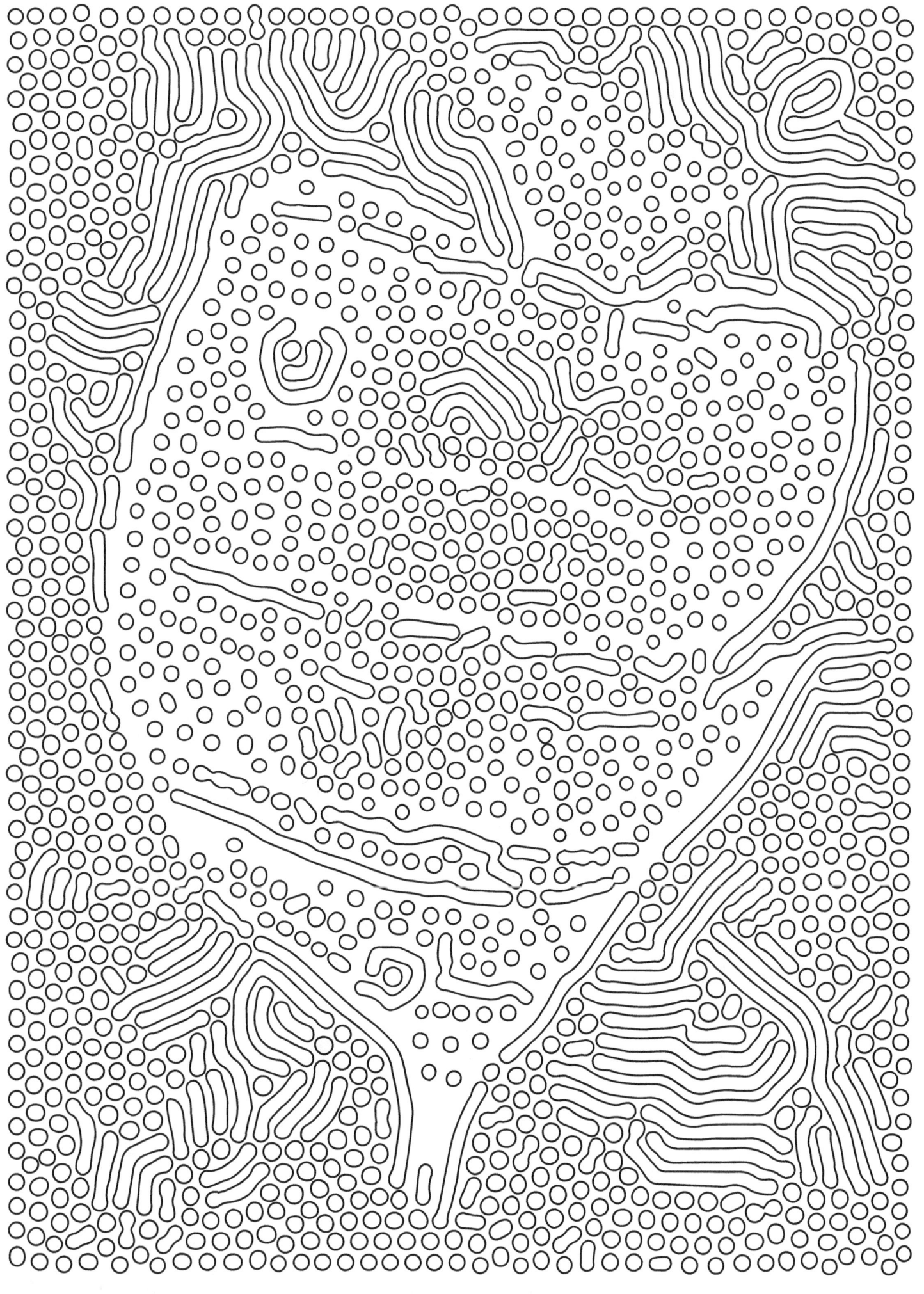

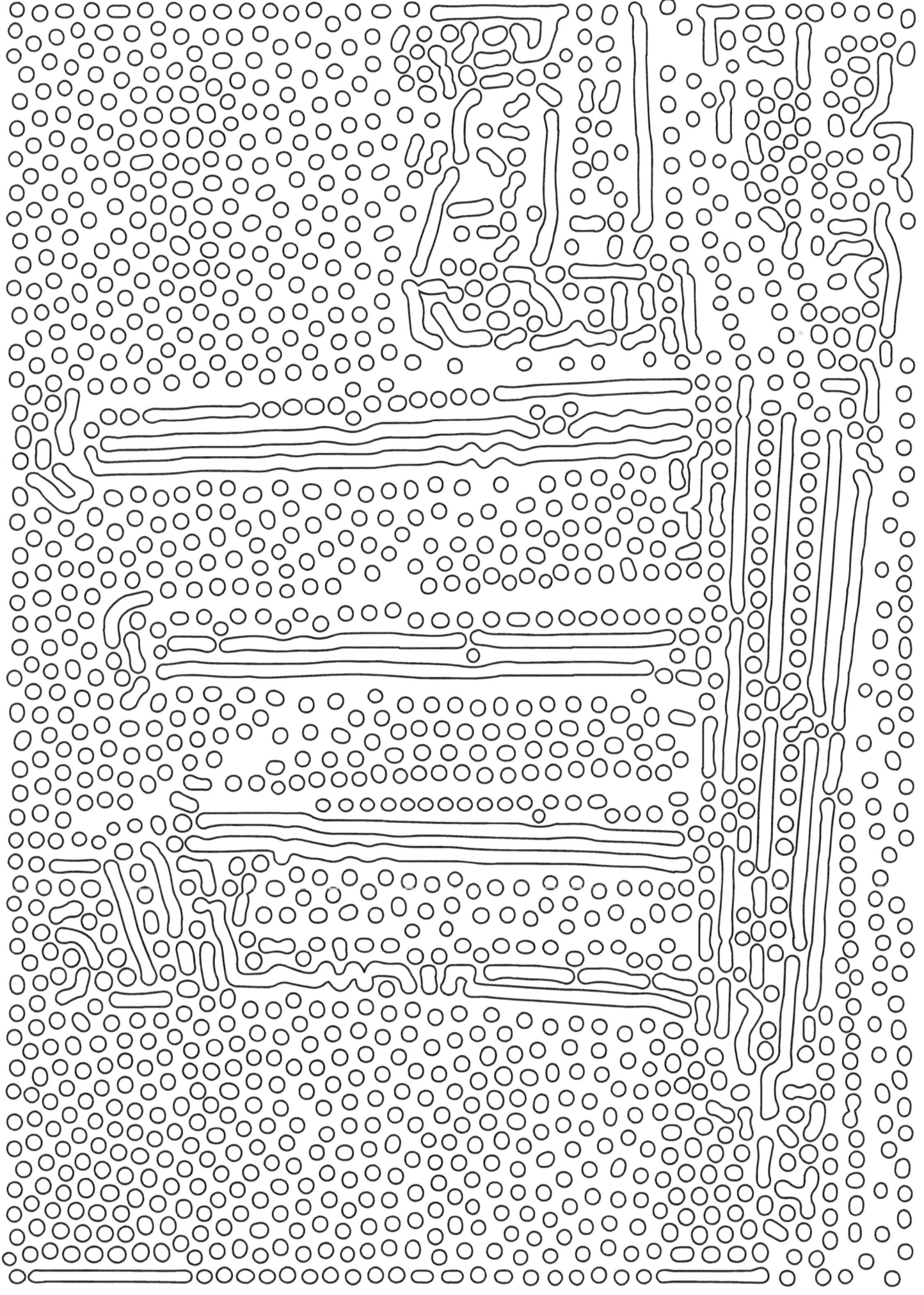

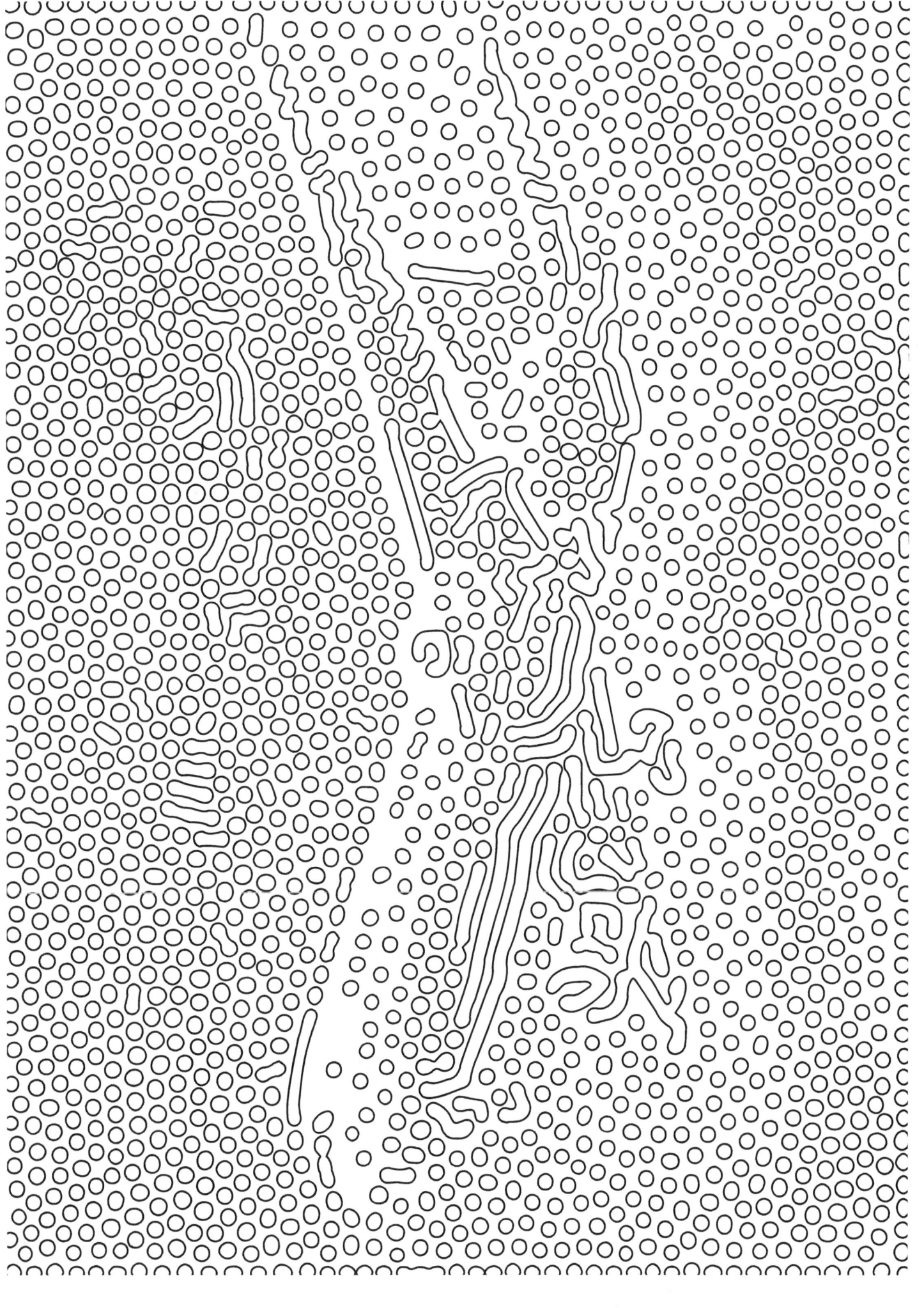

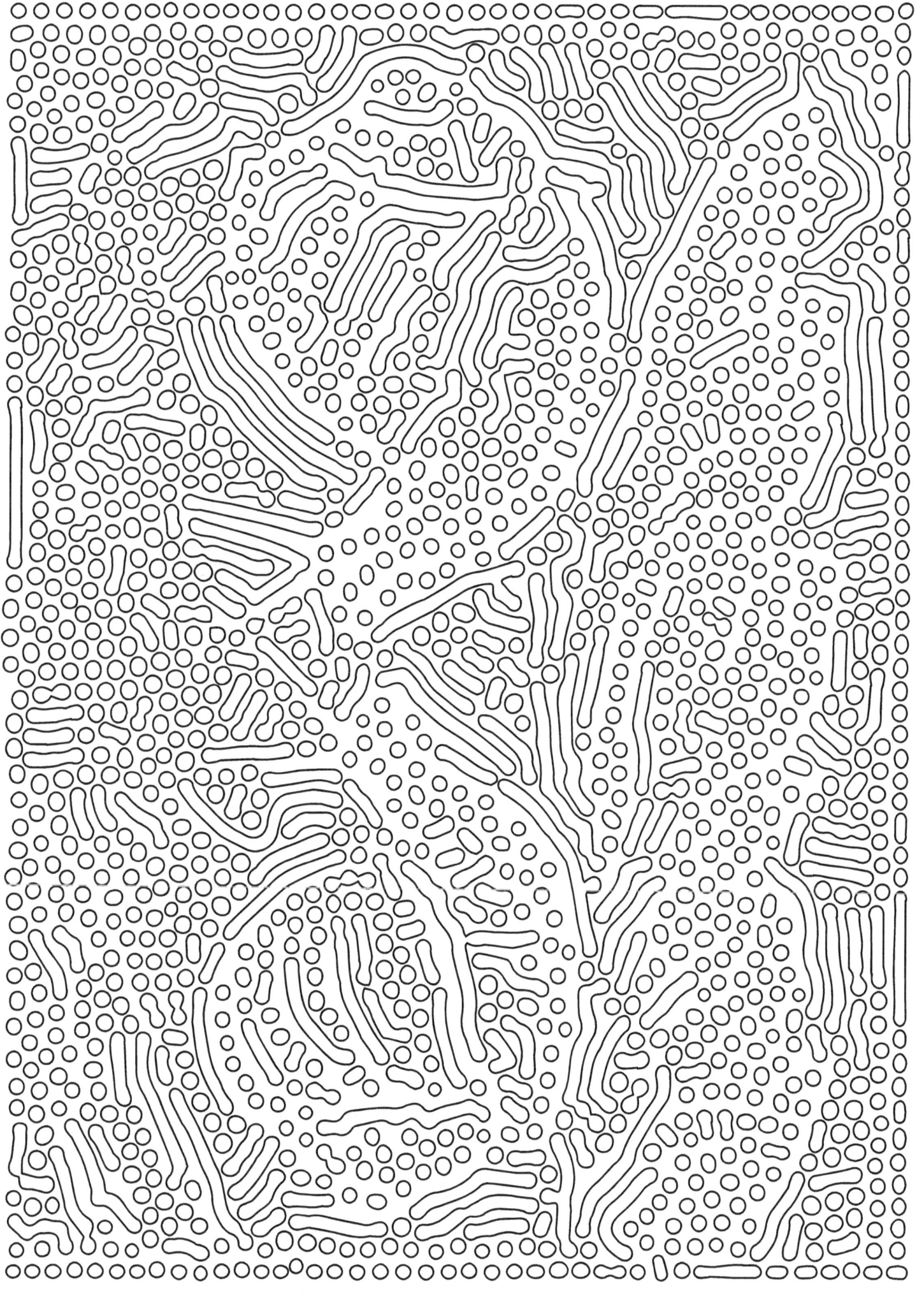

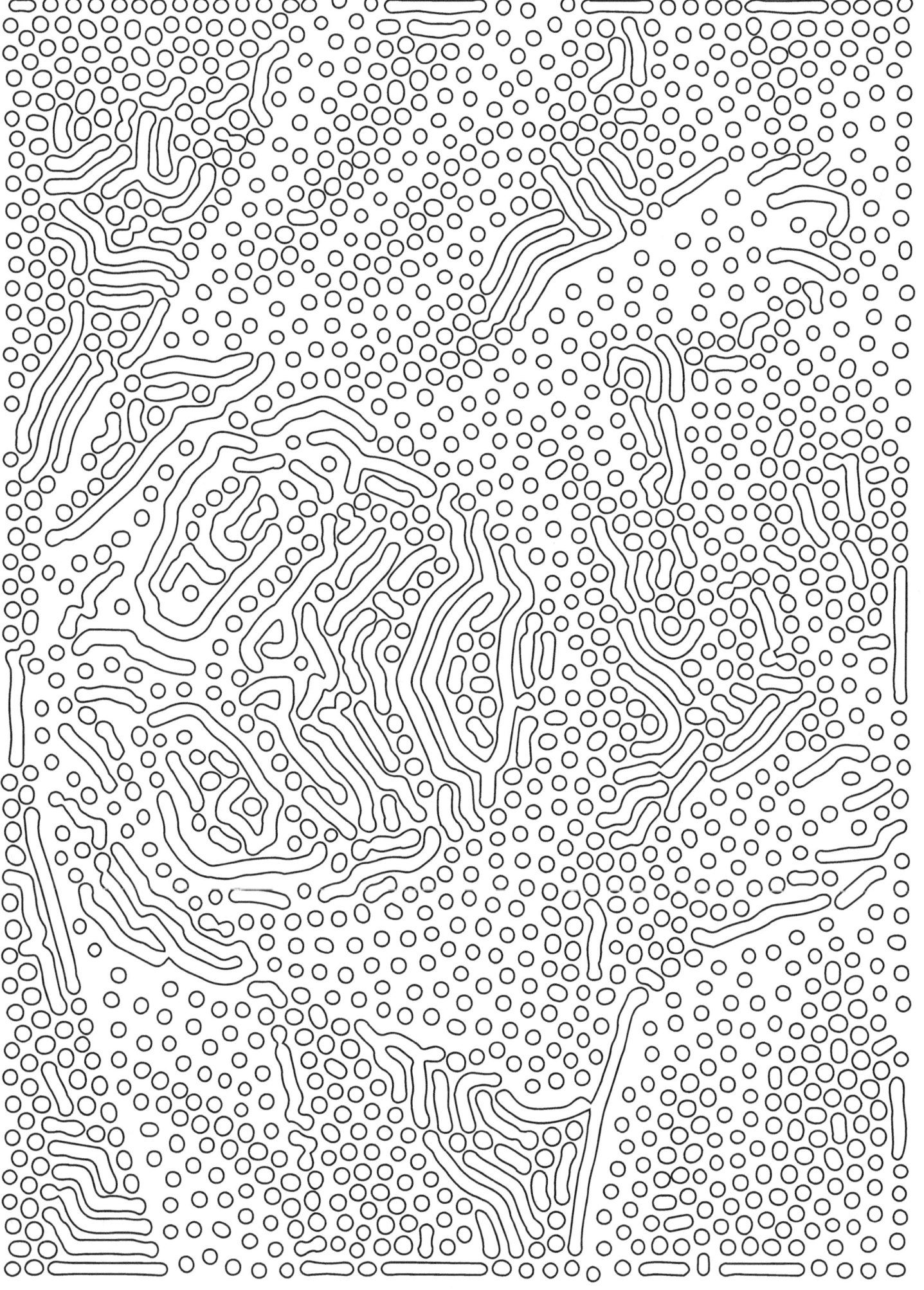

www.ingramcontent.com/pod-product-compliance
Lightning Source LLC
Chambersburg PA
CBHW081058240526
45465CB00025B/2675